To Dan.
Wh[illegible]t
one [illegible] of us on
Kingsbury Road.
Love, Ross

Climbing Pinnacle Hill

Tales about Becoming a Family Man

Ross Arkell Webber

To Mary Lou

"I remember you. You're the one who made my dreams come true, a few kisses ago...... When my life is through and the angels ask me to recall the thrill of it all, I shall tell them, I remember you."

Johnny Mercer

PREFACE

Pinnacle Hill can feel like a mountain when one is climbing it with four small children. And we were all dressed in Sunday-go-to-church clothes. After attending Mass in Hanover, New Hampshire where I was teaching a summer course at Dartmouth College, we returned to Lyme where we were staying. Our cabin overlooked Post Pond, but looming behind the cabin was The Hill. One can't see the peak from the lower level because of the dense forest, but friends had told us how great is the view of the Connecticut River Valley. So up we started up – a thirty four year old couple with four children aged eleven to four.

Of course it was dumb. The path was quite steep and muddy in places (not to mention, poison ivy danger on the lower reaches). Some of us fell several times. Yet, what an adventure it was! One of life's greatest. We reached the peak as a family, gloried in the view and this father felt like Edmund Hillary atop Everest. Ever since, we have tried to keep alive that spirit of adventure and family togetherness.

Forty years later when our 50th wedding anniversary was approaching, my wife and I decided it would be great to invite our children, their spouses and children to the same cabins to celebrate our good fortune. Twenty three of us gathered for a week, one day of which reenacted that Pinnacle Hill climb. The cover photograph shows us gathered around the peak's monument. It was an even greater experience to share it with most of my eighteen grandchildren – even if half of them had young legs that conveyed them to the top long before this Poppy/Granddad.

Climbing is an apt metaphor for the process of growing up, marrying, raising a family and learning how to be a husband and father. What follows is my exploration of how I more or less successfully navigated this climb. This is not a conventional autobiography so I wouldn't bore you with every meaningful episode. Nonetheless, I hope making this journey with me will help you to understand this writer's trip and, hopefully, gain insight into your own climb, from where you are coming and to where you may be going.

I owe thanks to my older brother Dick and younger brother Alan for their comments. We experienced some events similarly and others very differently. Most of all I am grateful to my wife Mary Lou who has shared in most of my life's adventure as well as read this manuscript multiple times.

Ross A. Webber. Haddonfield, New Jersey 2013

TABLE OF CONTENTS

ONE

The Vanished Webber Wealth

Webber family home in New Rochelle, NY 1908

My great grandfather Richard Webber spent his young life on a farm called Barton's Run in the Southwestern English province of Devonshire. At age 16 in 1863, he emigrated to the United States seeking work in New York City as a butcher's apprentice. He settled in

Harlem then still a semi-rural suburb to Manhattan. He prospered with the growing city and eventually opened his own butcher shop which grew into the Harlem Packing Company covering a full city block from Lexington to Third Avenues, 121 to 122 Streets. It billed itself as the largest retail butcher establishment in the country.

To ensure its source of supply, he established an office in Kansas near the stockyards and the railroad east. He also owned and operated a large poultry operation in Sioux City, Iowa. In time he was honored as Harlem businessman of the year, elected a Trustee of the Harlem Savings Bank and President of the Harlem Chamber of Commerce He built a family home at 1871 Madison Avenue near what is now Marcus Garvey Park.

As a business owner and manager he was a paternalist in the best sense. Contemporary observations repeatedly cite his concern for his 500 employees' welfare as manifest in his profit sharing (20% of annual profits distributed among all employees}, recreation outings, and welfare funds. He even had an employee council whose input was welcome. His management style was very creative for its time. Of course, none of this would meet modern expectations of union representation and collective bargaining, but for his times he was remarkably responsive to his employees. Simply assuming that his employees would be interested, the company paper HRH featured stories of his many trips to England with his wife and children. His oldest son's (Richard, Jr.) attendance at Sheffear College in England was dutifully reported. In retrospect, attempting to raise his son as an English gentleman was a mistake – as we will see.

The founding Richard died at sea on the *SS St. Louis* in 1907 while returning from his annual trip to England "to ease his hay fever." The death was widely reported in world newspapers and I have many yellowing obituary reports. Particularly appealing to the papers was that he left $500 (approximately $10,000 in today's dollars) to each of his employees out of an estate valued at $7,000,000.00 ($160,000,000 today). It is not a huge amount in today's hedge fund environment, but it certainly cast a spell on Webber family lore. That spell continues when one visits the mausoleum that he built in Kensico Cemetery in upstate New York. It is a mini-Greek temple on a hillside overseeing a long valley. Three generations of Richard Webbers and spouses are interred there. The very concept is difficult to understand today. Yet, when we recently visited the site, one could see that another generation of newly rich are following my great grandfather's vision. Among the older WASP crypts are newer, flashier monuments with laser etched portraits of their Asian-American occupants.

Two sons and a daughter survived Richard Sr. and they inherited the company. In time the two sons bought out their sister's share and then apparently ran the business into the ground. Parts were sold to the Swift Packing Company, but the Harlem location was liquidated in 1919. Those of us in the later generations often wondered why. And where had the money gone?

Perhaps Richard Senior's passing freed up his son to pursue the then 1908 fashionable movement out of New York City to New Rochelle, a Westchester County community on Long Island Sound just north of the City. Settled by French Huguenot refugees, New Rochelle was nicknamed "Queen City of the Sound" and it was becoming a haven for newly prosperous business and entertainment figures. Frank Gilbreth of "time motion" and the film "Cheaper by the Dozen" fame and Eddy Foy of Broadway and "The Three Little Foys" were new residents. The George M. Cohan song "Forty Five Minutes from Broadway" described the city and E. L. Doctorow captured the town and era in his novel RAGTIME. It was the home of Laura and Rob Petrie in the 1960's television classic, "The Dick Van Dyke Show."

I was born in 1934 so I knew my grandfather Richard Jr. only when I was a small child. I knew his younger brother William for much longer. With little interest in running the packing house, they pursued more intellectual pursuits. William became a respected cryptologist whom I well remember living in his older brother's home holed up in his third floor room working away on vast sheets of paper filled with numbers (not unlike the garage scene in the film "A Beautiful Mind"). Was he a secret agent? Did he suffer from some mental illness? Probably, but it was obscured by his chronic alcoholism. His brother Richard Jr. pursued a more traditional life as a suburban family gentleman with a deep interest in local and national history. He wrote many articles and received several honors from historical associations

Although my father, Richard III, was born in 1902 in the family home at Madison Avenue and 121st Street, from the age of six he lived in a big white corner mansion on Hamilton Avenue in New Rochelle. I remember many visits to that house with its *port cohere*, three floors, seemingly endless bedrooms, built-in vacuum system, and chauffer and cook's quarters over the two and a half car garage. The Philippine house couple used to make me peanut butter and mint jelly sandwiches (a favorite still today). My grandmother dressed like the dowager Lady Crawley in Masterpiece Theatre's "Downton Abbey." She always insisted on (painfully) cleaning my finger nails while offering me lessons on etiquette. My grandfather would receive the roast beef set before him by the butler and carve our portions at the table.

My youthful memory is of a home filled with a strange set of multi-generation family members. On the third floor lived an elderly lady called Grandma Jordan (Richard Sr.'s widow, Lucy Jordan) and the reclusive Great Uncle Will. On the second floor lived my two aunts. Aunt Julie was my father's older sister who had graduated from Smith College, never married, loved books, played golf and affected an avant-garde style evocative of Katherine Hepburn. Her younger sister Marguerite (Aunt Midge), was a beautiful finishing school graduate and aspiring actress. Her husband Ross Walker had died of a burst appendix. Since my mother was her best friend, I was named after him. And of course also in the big house was my Nana sometimes called Grandma Carroll (Richard Jr.'s widow Julia Carroll). From my perspective of almost 70 years later, it all seems like the film "The Family Tennenbaum."

The most important occupant of the mansion for me was none of the above however. She was Midge's daughter, my cousin Rita. A year older than I, she and I were close friends and fellow conspirators who spied on every corner of the big house. After almost being caught experimenting with smoking cigarettes (which everyone else in the house consumed with abandon), Rita and I dropped the still hot matches and cigarettes into the century old grandfather clock in the front hall. We soon had a smoking hole in the clock and the floor under it. In later years we went swimming together, mercilessly killed frogs, drove her jeep through muddy fields, rode her horse "Flicka", and listened to every Sigmund Romberg operetta. She tried to teach me the succession of British Kings and Queens and the reasons why females got "the curse." For a time, she was my best pal.

I think that Richard Senior's two sons, Richard Junior and William were seduced by the "English disease." Their father rose from humble butcher's boy roots but the two sons admired British country squires, aspiring to the life of country gentlemen. Being professional was passé; becoming an amateur scholar-explorer the objective. They sold the business and retired. The retired gentleman's life, however, consumed more money than was coming in from investments. Perhaps not paying sufficient attention to those investments in October 1929 contributed to the problem.

After my grandfather Richard Jr.'s death in 1938, all of the white mansion's inhabitants remained until the older ones died off. My father Richard III had married my mother Muriel in 1928 actually eloping from the Webber house while she was visiting his sister Midge. My older brother Richard IV was born in 1929, I in 1934, James Bruce in 1940, Robert Alan in 1945, Janet Emily in 1946 and Muriel Lynn in 1953. My father, the rich man's son, had attended Steven's Institute of Technology where he trained in electrical engineering and the emerging field of electronics. He was a whiz at repairing radios and that became his first business in a little shop near his family home in New Rochelle. It was in a lovely strip of pseudo-Spanish shops near the entrance to the elegant Rochelle Park.

Unhappily, during the Great Depression not enough people were buying radios so the shop failed. Seeking another opportunity (and perhaps looking for more opportunity to go fishing), the then family of four moved to Daytona Beach, Florida. I think everyone loved it there except me. I found Florida very hot and humid with huge bugs. Still I fondly remember riding in the car as my Dad drove on the sandy beach in and out of the waves. Afterwards, we would stop and eat watermelons (which all my life I have remembered as emblematic of our being poor).

When my grandfather Richard Jr. died, we moved north again to New Rochelle where my parents rented two places before buying their first house in a nice but more modest neighborhood than his boyhood home.

His job prospects, however, were not improved and he took an hourly paid position in a repair shop in Scarsdale. Virtually every day, my mother would pile the, by then, three kids in the car and we would drive Dad to work and then pick him up.

His career future improved when a friend suggested he apply to William Paley's growing Columbia Broadcasting System. That succeeded and Dad spent almost thirty years with WCBS in New York City, mainly in master control where he made the second by second connections that brought voices to radios all over the world. Colleagues whom he admired were Edward R. Murrow, Frank Stanton, and Eric Severeid. I particularly remember how angry he was that he was forced to become a member of the United Electrical, Radio and Machine Workers of America (UE), especially when they called a strike in 1950 which he refused to observe. He was labeled a "rat," but

William Paley did treat us to Christmas dinner at a Brass Rail restaurant in New York City.

Growing up I generally had the erroneous notion that our immediate family was quite poor, especially in comparison with the big mansion and my grandparents' past. I frequently heard hushed conversations about unpaid bills and store credit was sometimes refused when we ordered groceries or tried to buy gasoline. Years later I became aware that they were not the best money managers. And looking back, I think they (and me) must have been subsidized by my grandfather's estate. Sometime in the 1950's I saw a pay chit that suggested that my father's annual salary didn't exceed $6000 (about $50,000 today). My mother never had a paying job until after Dad died. I remember a lawyer Walter Spooner periodically coming to the house on behalf of the Webber Estate and the Irving Trust Company.

The myth of past wealth affected some of us quite adversely. My cousin Rita, who had grown up living in the big house, complained about the unfairness of all that wealth disappearing. Since outsiders often thought our family was wealthy and in our view we were not, some of us complained of fate's inequity. Our generation should have been rich too! What self-centered, self-pitying crybabies we were. I disagree with the choices made by my grandfather Richard Junior and Uncle Will, but it was their decision. They had no obligation to provide for me. Of course, I still sometimes wish that they had.

When my mother died in 1990 in the nursing home at New Rochelle Hospital, she was broke. The last $8000 of stock was spent on her death and burial. Aunt Hattie, Richard Junior's sister who in 1908 had sold out to her brothers, had her money wisely invested elsewhere and died a multi-millionaire in a lovely Scarsdale Spanish style home whose beautiful tile floors and indoor fountain I still fondly recall. I did benefit from one segment of old Webber money however: when my Aunt Julie died unmarried and childless, she left her money to her siblings' children. My share in 1982 was $30,000 and it was most gratefully received. I bought a Boston Whaler boat.

Webber Mausoleum, Kensico Cemetery, Valhalla, NY

"Ross, why did you people give it all away?" The question was posed by a much older Wharton Professor colleague William Gomberg, son of Jewish immigrants from Russia. The "you people" referred to were not any of today's noteworthy minorities. Rather Bill saw me as representative of yesterdays' power wielders - White Anglo Saxon Episcopalians. And I was. Bill, I think, was a little surprised to discover Jews like himself becoming so respected and successful in breaking down the exclusionary glass ceilings that theretofore had kept "his people" down at prestigious universities. His way had been that of the 1930's: CCNY and organizing with the Ladies Garment Workers Union. He was familiar with picket lines and strike breaking goons. Now here he was a respected author and full professor in the Ivy League whose comments were frequently solicited by the press.

In Bill's world view, WASPS like myself had dominated American affairs by virtue of privileged access to top universities like Princeton and Columbia and inherited wealth (unfortunately not true in my case, but only because I missed by two generations). Bill's rhetorical question asked why "we" hadn't fought harder to hold on to our privileged positions. My grandfather's decisions suggest the answer to the question.

TWO

Poor and Rich in School

Stephenson Elementary School, New Rochelle, NY

"The School is gone, but the rock is still there." So I was told recently by a woman whom I didn't recognize. But I immediately remembered the rock. It was outside of the Stephenson School perched on a small hill in New Rochelle, New York. The rock has a low metal fence along the top, but seventy years ago one could walk out of the school, climb on the rock and survey the playground some twenty five feet below. It was thrilling to the five and six year old that I was when I attended the school.

My erstwhile kindergarten classmate elicited my earliest memory of that year. I am sitting on a chair in the hall outside of my classroom. I am being punished and my banishment is intended to embarrass me because my mouth has been covered with an adhesive bandage – a sort of public stockade. I can't talk. The punishment seems to have been merited because I don't recall being angry and I don't think my parents were particularly upset. Can you imagine what the response would be today? I was banished for kissing too many of the girls in class (and I hope at least talking to them beforehand). Luckily, I was never sent to a psychiatrist for an analysis of my premature attempts at being amorous. I must have gained control over such inappropriate behavior because I never again provoked such discipline. However, I still enjoy kissing.

After my year in first grade, my parents purchased their first home and we moved to a more affluent New Rochelle neighborhood and I transferred to the second grade at the Henry Barnard School. We weren't rich in the modern sense of the term. To the extent we kids even thought about it, we saw our Barnard School group as strictly middle class. We sure weren't as rich as the kids from the north end of New Rochelle near Wykagyl Country Club. Still, even in the 1940's nearly all of the parents of my Barnard friends were college graduates. They were lawyers, physicians, business owners, etc. And many of us were invited to join the prestigious dancing class at the North Avenue Presbyterian Church which was one of the first public indicators of social status. Our Barnard classmates from City Park were not invited.

The school was located in a beautiful English Tudor building at the foot of an impressive hill between the two areas from which it drew students. We lived on the top of the hill just off of the ambitiously named "Mountain Avenue", in an area named "Larchmont Woods" to give it status by association with its neighboring even wealthier Town of Larchmont. Parallel to Mountain was "Forest Avenue" and our homes were sited in the woods in between. The contrast with the poorer City Park was dramatic, with a kind of Dickensian flavor.

On the mountain top we used to play a lot of basketball, usually in recessed driveways that produced scraped knuckles when we drove to the basket from the side. We did put up a freestanding basketball backboard on a cul-de-sac on which the homes had never been completed, but it was only usable in good weather. What we wanted was access to the Barnard school gym. It was not available in the evenings or on the weekends. We went to the Principal with a petition. Our core complaint was the "poor" kids in West New Rochelle had an indoor court in the Boys Club or YMCA which were much too far away for us to travel. At first we were rebuffed with explanations of heating and janitorial costs, etc., but eventually we were given Saturday morning access. So we were successful social activists at age 12! Heady stuff.

We decided to make another request. We had heard about school dances in other parts of town so we asked the Principal for our own Saturday night dance (we had several Jewish kids in the group and it couldn't be on Friday night). An evening weekend event was rejected, but the administration compromised on a weekday afternoon "Tea Dance." None of us had ever heard of the term, but we saw it as a good offer.

Negotiating with that Principal taught me an important lesson about leadership that was helpful in later life. He had been a teacher at Barnard before serving in the Army Air Corps as a bombardier during World War Two. When he came back to visit the school as the war was ending, he wore his uniform decorated with ribbons. Well, we boys were mesmerized. When he returned to teaching and subsequently to Principal, he came with great political capital. He didn't have to listen to our schoolboy "demands." But he did with seriousness and respect.

Although I'm sure he was under some administrative, teacher and parental pressures, he never conveyed a message that change was impossible or that we had no right to complain. Most of all, he didn't seem to feel that his authority was threatened by his negotiation with twelve year olds. Confidence in one's self and situation is imperative in being an effective negotiator.

Alas, I didn't always live up to his example in my later senior management positions.

Dressing for the dance produced a controversy. Some of the girls had started to stuff their bras with Kleenex to reduce the appearance gap with some of their earlier maturing classmates. Indeed. I had been soundly slapped in class by one of the most developed girls when I inadvertently (yes, I'm sure it was by accident) turned and my arm brushed her prominent breasts. Although why is still unclear to me sixty five years later, some of my friends were upset about the tissue stuffing. Opposed to false advertising? Confusing signals? Too much temptation for twelve year olds? Some boys seemed to think that the "nicer girls; were mainly in the delayed development crowd so the bra stuffing implied that the nice girls were moving into the faster group. Perhaps this scared the more conservative boys. I was asked to intervene with the nice girl leadership to see if the augmentation could be curtailed. Why me? I guess I was seen as a conservative popular with friends in all groups. Whatever. It was the first of many mediation assignments in my life.

Clearly my fledgling political skills failed me the day I was beaten up by a girl. I was 10 when one of the City Park Black kids called me out over a slight of how the class had responded to the 1944 death of Franklin D. Roosevelt. Reflecting the views of some conservative parents, some white students cheered when the news was announced in class. I absolutely was not among them given that my parents admired FDR who was my personal hero for many years. Nonetheless, I was the target. Since I was one of the slow to maturers and she was among the earliers, she was much taller and heavier than I was. And Elsie hit me so fast that I was never even confused about whether I should strike a girl. I had no chance to throw a punch; I just went into what was later called a Mohammed Ali "rope-a-dope" and took my pounding.

Today there is much discussion about the lifelong impact of great teachers on a child's career success. I don't know if my fifth grade teacher Mrs. Grant was a great teacher or not, but I do remember that she thought I was great. It was my first experience with someone thinking that I was really smart. I guess I thought I was, but here was a teacher who told me that I "could become anything I wanted to be." Surely it was a cliché and I have no idea whether she differentiated between me and any others, but it was tremendously motivating. And thankfully, my grades seem to validate her judgment – in everything except spelling.

I had a mental block with spelling. I believe it stemmed from my inability to sound out syllabi. I had learned to read very young by memorizing the appearance of words. When faced with the word that I had not seen, I could not visualize it so my spelling would be wildly inaccurate. I could live with this in private with bad marks on my papers, but I was subject to public embarrassment through the torture of spelling bees. And worse, team spelling bees started when the best two spellers were named team captains who then publicly chose their teams. The first few times I was picked based on friendship, but my abysmal performance soon led me to be selected down with the slowest of classmates. It was humiliating. I remember failing my team when I couldn't spell the first word asked: "lettuce." I was just lucky to have other subjects where my skills could be demonstrated.

Books and the town library played such a big role in my early life. I read continuously. The main public library was three bus rides away, but there was a small branch overlooking the lovely twin lakes in front of New Rochelle High School. It was about two miles away and required changing the bus once. I spent many hours in the second floor reading room. My primary school reading was weighted heavily toward nature based books. I read Eric Knight's LASSIE COME – HOME, Albert Payson Terhune's LAD: A DOG stories as well as Ernest Thompson Seton's nature adventures including WILD ANIMALS I HAVE KNOWN. I was particularly attracted to stories in which an animal was the courageous hero including BIG RED, THE WALRUS KING, and Jack London's CALL OF THE WILD. At one point I wanted to become a taxidermist, perhaps so I could stop time and capture the spirit of the animals I admired.

I read also read about real people of course. Owen Johnson's STOVER AT YALE about the adventures of Dink Stover became a kind of guide for my twelve year self in how to become a self-reliant and ethical person in subsequent maneuvering through high school and college. I even applied to Yale when I was twelve years old. The admissions office kindly wrote back to tell me to apply again when I was a high school senior. Alas, by then my ambition had shifted to Princeton and F. Scott Fitzgerald's less admirable THIS SIDE OF PARADISE hero, Amory Blaine.

THREE

The Talking Woman

Muriel Arkels at seventeen

Our family of eight was gathered around the dining room table ready to begin the Thanksgiving dinner which was much delayed. Mom was drunk. Finally, my eight year old younger sister said to her, "You are like a person caught in a prison." It was an incredibly insightful observation.

To me when growing up, it seemed impossible that this amazing, beautiful and talented woman could so captured by alcohol. At the Atlanta High School for girls she had been president of the thespian society and voted "Best Looking" by her classmates. Supposedly, the men at Georgia Tech had named her "Miss Georgia Peach." She lived on West Peachtree Street. Years later as a married matron in New Rochelle, New York she was even more successful, reaching the political and social pinnacle. Even the city's then legendary mayor would hit on her. In my senior year in high school, she pulled off the ultimate positional coup: President of the New Rochelle High School Parent

Teachers Association AND President of the New Rochelle Hospital League for Service. I remember her looking radiant on the school's theater stage introducing Vaughn Monroe and his Orchestra on the night of the League's Annual fund raising concert. "Racing with the Moon" indeed.

I have never seen another as effective on the telephone which was constantly at her ear (how she would have loved today's smart phones!). She was forever organizing events, especially her ladies poker games. She had an elaborate set of chips which would go flying across our dining room table almost as fast as her friend's words. I loved watching them because in those days the women all dressed up with lovely clothes and expert makeup. Some were almost competitive with my mother.

And yet. Many days I would come home from school afraid that I would find her passed out on the couch. Or worse, that she would be awake and still drinking and smoking. The cigarettes and coffee often were consumed even faster than the drinks. Sixty years later, my stomach still churns as I recall those moments.

Even worse, however, were the days when she would endeavor to maintain family routine while she was secretly nipping from a hidden bottle. We children were of course exquisitely sensitive to the telltale behaviors betraying her efforts at secrecy. As such occasions were repeated, I was struck with how the time and drinks to intoxication grew ever shorter. It simply took less alcohol.

Only many years later did I become aware of diagnoses such as clinical depression or bi-polar disorder (formerly manic-depressive). I now know that alcoholism and bi-polarism are strongly correlated, especially if a parent were alcoholic. And Mom's father had a severe drinking problem for many years. So did my older brother. I wasn't aware of how serious it was until the day I was asked to pick him up at his college to bring him home for Christmas vacation. My girlfriend and I drove up. On the trip home of about five hours, he and his roommate stopped every half hour or so at wayside bars that seemed to appeal to them. We sat in the car while they had a few drinks while playing darts and then returned to the car. It was a horror. And it only escalated for him in future years.

I never saw my mother in an obviously manic phase, but her incredible energy and ability to go with little sleep may have been surrogates. She could smoke and read the night away and our home was overflowing with books. When she died and we cleaned out her apartment, the nicotine coated books were shelved three deep.

When she was in the hospital dying of emphysema and lung cancer, I asked about her deep addiction to cigarettes. She replied that she started as a teenager in anger toward her father; saying, "Every cigarette was a nail in his coffin." I assume the depth of her anger stemmed from her father's drinking and treatment of her mother. He was simply unreliable and sometimes verbally abusive. As a traveling salesman he never bought a house and seldom even rented an apartment. He and his wife lived in hotels. When desperate, he and my maternal grandmother would move into our house. My younger brothers would often be bumped from their room.

While in his daughter's home, he would frequently attempt to impose his own conservative views on the family. Although born in Canada, he was a transplanted Southerner reflecting mid-twentieth century racial attitudes. He would walk out of the room when a black (not his term) like Nate King Cole appeared on the screen. This was anathema to my mother. Whether in rebellion or by conviction she was a liberal with a capital L. She was devoted to equality and freedom. Never did we hear racial slurs or discriminatory remarks in our house. Her every manner (including "honeys and "darlings" to all) communicated inclusion.

Her devotion to personal autonomy extended to her treatment of her children, or at least me. No rules were imposed. I was encouraged to make my own behavioral decisions. When I was applying to college I never consulted my parents about schools or informed them to which I was applying. I felt good about this and appreciative of the autonomy given to me. I hope my parents didn't feel neglected.

My father died when my mother was fifty-eight. Her life then miraculously turned around. With her oldest son's example and encouragement, she became active in Alcoholics Anonymous. After consuming five and a half cans of a six pack of beer, she deposited the last can down on the steps to a Long Island treatment center and never had another drink. She got a job in a mail and telephone marketing firm where her interpersonal skills brought her instant success. Freed of the burdens of young children and with her parents both dead and her husband gone, she lived what appeared to be one of the happiest periods of her life. It would take more of a psychologist than me to explain this transformation, but it was heartening to me.

The smoking never stopped however – not until the final diagnosis. As the only non-smoker in the family, I continued to have problems with it. Was it the smoking itself that bothered me? I don't think so. Rather, the smoking was so associated with the earlier drinking years. I wanted to avoid the memories. I recognize now that, even in my 50's, I simply lacked the courage. To my shame, for twenty years I

abdicated virtually all communications with my Mom to my wife. But, she brightened my mother's life.
I was the last of the family to be with Mom in the nursing home on the day she died. She of course was old and her body wrecked by the cancer. Yet, lying in her bed, her face still retained its amazing beauty. I even told her that she had the most perfectly shaped nose that I had ever seen. What a strange thing to say at such a time. Perhaps I just wanted to hold on to the image of the one facial feature that time and illness could not touch.

She was very restless and kept trying to get up, but she fell and badly gashed her leg. The nurses came in to apply a dressing and I had to leave. I just sensed that after I left they were going to tie her to the bed. But I left anyway and she died that night. So another regret was added to my overlong list.

At Mom's funeral, my older brother and I both spoke. He recited Reinhold Niebuhr's serenity prayer adopted by Alcoholics Anonymous which meant so much to both of them: "God, grant me the serenity to accept the things I cannot change. Courage to change the things I can. And wisdom to know the difference." I said that my mother was the smartest person I ever met. Her formal education ended with high school but her constant reading added a lot to that. More fundamentally, she just knew about people and life, even if she was not always able to handle or own. But when she was on the top of her game, she was the best. Some people can strike up a conversation with a stone. Mom could romance a stone wall.

FOUR

The Silent Man

Richard Webber III at age three

My father and I exchanged so few words. I have long wondered why. We never quarreled. I never rebelled. He was usually kindly and soft spoken. He rarely lost his temper, but when he did it was quick and explosive. Recently my ten year younger brother told me of his lifelong wish to be different than our Dad whom he saw as a passive quiet Milquetoast who made little impact on the world. My mother would complain that Dad was indecisive, reluctant to express his preferences on anything – even food which really bugged his wife. I cannot recall ever being disciplined at home. I can't even recall any stated rules. Friends to whom I describe this are incredulous. Their memories of their fathers are usually of a powerful, even frightening authoritarian who laid down the rules and that was that.

My Dad was extremely smart and well educated as an electrical engineer at Stevens Institute. He worked as a radio engineer at the Columbia Broadcasting System in New York City for 27 years. He made and operated his own short-wave radio station in the bedroom (it was taken away by the FBI shortly after the beginning of World War II). Post war, he built the first TV on our street with a tiny screen around which we would gather to watch granny images of professional wrestling and Milton Berle.

Right after the war he bought a small 14 foot molded plywood outboard motor boat. It was formed with a novel manufacturing technique derived from aircraft that created a small craft of lovely contours with a lighter weight than traditional frame and plank construction. The first motor was a small 3 horsepower Evinrude that moved the little boat surprisingly well even in a choppy Long Island Sound. In those days one had to remove the motor after each use to flush the salt water in a barrel of fresh water. At age twelve, I remember my semi-crippled Father struggling to remove and carry the engine from boat to barrel to storage locker.

Dad was very short and slight, perhaps five foot three inches in height. My mother was five foot six and she looked so much bigger. Part of his height challenge certainly was genetic stemming from the Devonshire farming stock that were his ancestors. Another contributor was his youthful polio which he contracted as a teenager. It left his legs sharply shrunken with a decided weakness and limp in his left one. It was agony watching him walk for any distance. But I never heard him complain or even joke about his condition. Because his around the clock radio job was considered critical by Washington, during World War Two he was granted a preferential gasoline rationing card. Nonetheless, sometimes there was no fuel and he would trudge down from our mountain to the Larchmont railroad station for the train to Grand Central.

Fishing was a great love for Dad. He tied his own flies and made lures that helped him fishing for flounder in the Sound, for striped bass off of Montauk, weakfish and tarpon in Florida. When out fishing, his total focus was on the contest with the fish. When we lived in Daytona Beach, one day he swam out to a sandbar perhaps a hundred years out in the ocean. There, he could stand closer to the deeper water and the fish. The tide was coming in, however, and in time he was overwhelmed by the waves and a rip tide. Calmly, he began to swim with the tide several hundred yards until he was clear to turn shoreward – all the time still carrying his fishing rod.

My older brother Dick loved fishing with him. In contrast, I found it boring. Shortly after he bought the runabout in 1946, I was with him preparing the boat at the public marina in Hudson's Park. Two tough looking men were loudly conversing some distance away, but easily overheard. As I recall, one said to the other: "So I hit the bitch and told her to shut her trap – I 'd had it with her complaining. I grabbed her hair and

………….." in words not fit to print. My father never said a word during the man' soliloquy. Afterwards he quietly said to me, "See what you can learn when you listen."

I sometimes think my father was more an observer of life than a participant. But then I had experienced none of the challenges that he had. I still regret that I never learned to fish, particularly when I didn't have much knowledge to pass on to my own children when they asked me to teach them to fish.

A couple of years later, he bought a 24 foot Chris Craft cruiser that held the whole family. He truly loved commanding the boat as we crossed Long Island Sound to Sands Point. Long Island. He would dive off the boat and swim ashore with the amazingly powerful arm strokes that many polio victims developed. When I painted a posthumous portrait of him sitting in his CBS office, I included his ever-present cigarette, his trusty

Leica along with the big clock and pictures of his boyhood home, a Christ Craft advertisement and a poster recommending fishing in Florida. My wife has suggested that he was a man who loved his toys. I had never seen it this way, but perhaps she was on to something. His fishing rods, short wave radio, cameras, sports car, two boats all represented toys to her. In looking back, he seemed to represent what we later came to call preppies with his Sperry topsiders and Orvis fishing jacket.

Dad was always a repairman and tinkerer. There was virtually nothing he wouldn't try to fix. He rarely called for help. This alleviated some of my guilt for misplacing his car keys in several critical instances. Once he drove me to LaGuardia airport when I was flying to a Navy assignment. I drove and then noticed as my plane was climbing that I still had the car keys in my pocket. I repeated the same error on my college graduation weekend when I took the train back to

Princeton; again with his keys in my pocket (can I spell ADD?). In both cases he was easily able to jump the cables on his 1951 Hudson. It would be a bit more difficult today.

I often wondered about that Hudson. It seemed to be so boring a car. But I recently toured the NASCAR Museum in Charlotte where I discovered to my surprise that the 1950's Hudson was the hottest car on the track in those years. In the winter of 1954 I borrowed the family Hudson to drive with a friend to visit our girlfriends at Wells College in Aurora, New York on Lake Cayuga. Late on a very snowy night we were speeding westward from Ithaca on the last leg of the trip hoping to reach the girls before midnight when they would be locked in for the night. The snow was deepening, however, and building up on the car's underside. The accelerator pedal became stuck to the floor. I turned to my equally impatient companion, Dave, and calmly asked him to reach down and pull the accelerator up. He did so and promptly pulled the pedal right out of the floor. Holding it in his hand, he asked me what to do with it. We didn't crash, but we didn't make it to the college in time. The girls simply waived to us from their dorm window. Such was life in the repressed 1950's.

My Dad's pride and joy, was a Jaguar XK, long hood and all. It once threw a rod blowing a hole in the side of the block. He changed that engine working in a dimly lit garage with a jury-rigged overhead block and tackle. I still wonder that he didn't kill himself. Much earlier in his married life, he almost did. He was an early rocketeer. Experimenting with mixing rocket fuel in a rented apartment before I was born, an explosion tore off half of his left hand including much of his thumb and pointer. For years he would frighten young children with a trick of "losing" his thumb. Still, I loved the big picture books he gave me on the solar system and flights to the moon illustrated by

Willy Ley's fantastic paintings. But it was the art more than the science that captured me.

Because of his avoidance of parties, friends thought my father was a bit of a snob. I think he was just shy because of his short stature and physical handicap. Seeing how extremely shy was one of my daughters gave me some awareness of its impact on behavior. Some people, of course, just need less social time because they are content to spend more time alone, which he did. This led to his wife regretting the time parties that she had to attend alone!

Unfortunately, Dad frequently started projects that were never finished. When the house became crowded with, eventually, six children, he started to renovate the attic into a bedroom with lovely pine paneling. But it was never finished. When my older brother left for college and then the Army and I for college and the Navy, the need to complete the project evaporated.

Dad suffered from serious abdominal problems, mainly ulcers. His heavy smoking and perhaps stressful work contributed to his illness. Following the medical protocol of the 1950's, he drank endless gallons of milk and eventually had a large portion of his stomach removed. Eating even very small portions of food became difficult. While he was still postoperative in New Rochelle Hospital, I pulled off one of the most self-centered and immature behaviors of my life. I persuaded my worrying mother to allow me to take the family car to drive up to Aurora to visit my girlfriend Mary Lou. And I did. It is testimony to the slow pace of my maturation that I was in my fifties and he was long gone before I even became aware of the callousness of my actions at nineteen.

For many years I was furious with Dad for not "disciplining" Mom over her drinking. I blamed him for her apparent unhappiness. Yet, for all his personal inadequacies, her problems were hardly his fault. As I later confronted psychological problems in my siblings, children and grandchildren, I realized how much depression and alcoholism were related to genetic predispositions beyond even a loving person's power to relieve.

My father died at 66 after only a year of retirement. He never seemed to make the transition from his clock based work environment to retirement's open time. He had served for many years Master Control Supervisor at the CBS headquarters in New York City. His job involved making sure that the multiple signals from around the world got to the proper stations and on the air at the correct time. It was a clock directed environment. The film about Edward R. Murrow, *Good Night and Good Luck,* accurately portrayed the controlled chaos of live broadcasting in the 1950's.

When he retired, Master Control's large sweep hand clock was removed and given to him (this was long before digital displays). I remember it on the wall in our home, but it no longer gave structure to his life. When he was still working, his great passion was fishing. From Long Island Sound, to Montauk on the Atlantic Ocean, to Tarpon Springs, Florida, seeking flounders, sea bass, tarpon or bonefish was the

Portrait of Richard Webber III in Master Control

anecdote to his clock stressed life. But after retirement, fishing lost its allure. It was attractive only in juxtaposition to work. Undoubtedly, unknown to me at the time he was already ill when he retired.

After his stroke, he was nearly blind and mute, so frustrated with his plight that he continually drummed his fingers on the hospital bed railing. He wanted out. A young cleric arrived at the door announcing his availability to give support and prayers. With visible irritation, my father waived him away. A committed non-believer to whom I told this tale said that my father was his hero for his death bed consistency. He died in a couple of days – an agnostic rationalist to the end. Perhaps my passion to BELIEVE is a backhanded gift from him.

I know little of my father's early experiences that might have contributed to his attitude. I know his mother was an adult convert to Roman Catholicism and I was amazed to find a plaque in New Rochelle's Holy

Family Church commemorating a Webber gift to the church. Whether my grandfather Richard Jr. was happy about this is unknown. Perhaps because of the impact of polio on his life, my father he was angry at life's unfairness. But, he never spoke to me either of his illness or his religious beliefs. I must have felt early that I would have a different perspective. Was it just a revolt against my father that has led me to a committed Catholic Christian life even without a strong underlying faith?

Commenting on Penn State's Joe Paterno's death, a Philadelphia sports writer observed that "after one's father dies, one's life is never the same." I feel so badly that this didn't seem to apply to me. Dad just had not been a big enough part of my life. I became essentially financially independent at 18 and had never needed financial support after college. I inherited neither money nor tangible goods. And yet, as I've indicated, so much changed with my Mom. And this provided me with great satisfaction. Nonetheless, as the years have passed, I miss what never was ever more. I am astounded to realize that when he died I was 34 years old and still too immature to really ask him about his life. Now nearing eighty, I know all the questions that I would like to talk about with him.

FIVE

Kisses, Strawberries and Henry Wallace

In 1947-1948 Henry Wallace was the darling of progressive Democrats. They had not forgiven Franklin Roosevelt for dumping his Vice President in favor of Harry Truman for the 1944 election. A third party was launched by Wallace Progressive admirers joined by various Socialists and a few Communists.

Two of his staunch supporters were the parents of an eighth grade classmate who was, more or less, my thirteen year old girlfriend. They were uneasy Jewish suburban refugees from New York City with a strong concern about social and economic inequality that was beyond anything I had ever seen. If they had been around in 2011, I expect they would have joined the "Occupiers" down on Wall Street. It must have been unsettling for them to be living in affluent Westchester County. I assume they had moved out of the city in search of a better public education for their daughter.

Sandy was a short, dark haired peppy girl with a dramatic flair. Her father was a music arranger for the hit radio (later television) show "Your Hit Parade." We would listen to Dorothy Collins, Snooky Lanson and Giselle McKenzie belting out each week's top twenty songs ending with: “So long for a while; that’s all the songs for a while; so long to your Hit Parade and the songs that were picked to be played…”

As an adult she would pursue an acting career. In eighth grade we were both involved in school dramatics. I played the school teen heartthrob in a one act play "Teen Magic." She played the cheer leader (shades of "Glee"). I found her energetic perkiness very attractive. We went to the Rye Playland amusement park where we rode the Ferris wheel. We suffered from a bit of vertigo and to blot out the view we spent most of the ride kissing. One summer day we told Sandy’s mother that we were going to pick some fresh strawberries. She said that she could use them to make strawberry short cake. We really intended to find strawberries. But we didn’t. Our time alone was too intoxicating. We never got around to the picking.

A hundred or so kisses later, the sun was descending and we had no strawberries. We ran to the nearby Congress Food Market. Alas, they had only frozen berries. Hurrying back to Sandy's house with the icy package, we ran them under hot water to defrost and separate them into individual berries hoping that Sandy's mother wouldn't detect our deceit. We soon had many mutilated strawberries and we were awash with red stains. Luckily her liberal mom accepted our bizarre tale but with a warning not to tell Sandy's stepfather.

The beginning of the end of our relationship was probably attending those Wallace for President rallies. The zealous mob psychology was overwhelming; the hatred of those of differing economic class and political persuasion frightening. It disturbed my Roosevelt oriented world. I wanted out. And soon was.

SIX

Dream Girl

Winter Prom 1952

I can't believe I wasn't aware of her in eighth grade. From ninth on, however, she became the center of everything. My first sighting, as I remember it, was looking across the arc of the ninth grade chorus and seeing a face – a face so full of radiance, of good will, of comfort with herself and the world. She simply projected her trusting disposition and her own trustworthiness.

Her name was Mary Louise Foradora. She was not from an affluent section of town. Indeed, her father had died when she was very young and her mother worked full time. She was a latch key child before we knew of the term. Her home was a rented flat on the second floor of a two family house in a decidedly modest neighborhood. And yet, in style, speech and demeanor she projected conservative CLASS. I was amazed then and remain so today.

Of course her trusting outlook was naïve. People sometimes played good natured pranks on her. Yet she was a person who seemed to create her own social environment. Others seemed to rise to her level of moral and ethical standards. This was certainly true for me. I was sort of drifting to the prevailing ethos of whomever I was with. That continued with Mary Lou but in a better direction. Did I become a better person? Certainly not, but I was so afraid of losing her good will that I simply refrained from the drinking and partying that many were discovering in high school. And she simply rejected my weak efforts at kissing, necking, or (heaven forbid) petting. We didn't even kiss until her sixteenth birthday. We dated almost exclusively for eight years before we had sex on our wedding night. Seems quaint today, but what a solid start to a life together it provided.

Mary Lou went on to be a star in high school. She was the most popular girl: Secretary of the Class, Secretary of the Student Government, President of her sorority, business manager of the school newspaper and band twirler. She was elected to the National Honor Society and voted "most pull with the faculty." If she was the sun, I was more the moon, I was voted "best looking" so we made a great looking couple at every prom and dance. And we went to them all.

When we married three months after college graduation and started off on our honeymoon, I was repeatedly amazed that she already knew how to live, what to eat, and what not. She knew how to cook and I loved her results. In our first eight weeks together, I gained twenty pounds. More importantly, she knew how to pace one's life by balancing rhythms of activity. Many years later when I had achieved a modest celebrity, I was interviewed by a reported who asked whom I most admired. Dropping FDR into second place, without hesitation I replied "my wife." She was (is) psychologically the healthiest person that I have ever met. Years later at probably the lowest point of my life when I was blaming myself for a child's serious problems, she saved me. Her calm and reasoned rebuttal of my distorted analysis of the situation restored my equilibrium.

Of almost equal influence in my maturation was Mary Lou's mother, Mary Christine. Widowed at a young age, she manifested unwavering courage and confidence in her independence and self-reliance. As a young girl she was the oldest daughter in a family with six brothers. Her father was an old fashioned Italian who demanded that she stay home and help her mother in caring for everyone. Very pretty, at nineteen he was named "Miss New Rochelle." The prize was a brand new roadster. Her father insisted that she reject it because he considered it was unseemly for a girl.

Mary fought her father as strongly as she could. Forced to leave high school, she attended Butler's Business College in Bridgeport, Connecticut learning tying, shorthand and bookkeeping. These were the basic skills that enabled her to make her way for thirty years as the all-purpose receptionist-book keeper-business manager of a small printing business. From the beginning she accepted me as a fifteen old into her life as a friend of her daughter's. After working all week, she never wanted to stay home on Sundays and on many occasions I would ride in her Chevrolet coupe's back seat on visits to her family and favorite restaurants.

Eating at these restaurants broadened my till then very narrow spectrum of acceptable foods (not to mention my table manners). Mary also provided a lesson on how to drink alcohol. She would order a single Manhattan or Rob Roy which she clearly enjoyed. Unlike at home, I never had to worry that the drink would escalate into many leading to a messy ending. Many years later after Mary had lived with us for some time, I would come home from work and the three of us would sit on our porch discussing life and sipping our Manhattans. I cherish the memory of those evenings.

When Mary became gravely ill at age 94, her desire was to remain at home. We contacted a hospice service and she subsequently died in her bed in our home. Until two days before her death, she was still able to talk about her beloved Phillies and who they needed to strengthen their lineup. She greeted her first Great-Great Grandchild just days before she died. We were sitting by her as she passed. I told Mary Lou that I was so proud of what we had done. We had both tended to the oxygen, bathed her, changed under clothing and helped her to the toilet. Mary sometimes complained about her infirmities, but never did she curse the hand that life had dealt her. She believed in her Roman Catholic Christian faith as a child because, ultimately, there is no other way to believe.

Mary Lou and I have now been married over fifty seven years, but every day I look at her and see her as a seventeen year old presiding over one of the high school organizations that she led, looking smashing in her polka dotted organza shirtwaist dress so beautiful and so confident that she could handle whatever the world required. And she has, and does.

SEVEN

Driving Papa Jim

1948 Packard Clipper Sedan

In the summer of 1950 I turned sixteen, received my driving license and was given what I then thought was the best job in the world – driving my salesman grandfather's gorgeous Packard Clipper on a trip around his territory. I could barely see over the art deco chrome flying zephyr that served as a faux radiator cap. Her flying hair was always in my line of vision. I felt like Ben Hur steering his chariot.

Papa Jim, my grandfather, was a traveling salesman for the New York City luxury merchant Henri Bendel. He sold cosmetics, perfume and luxury accessories to boutiques all over the northeast. I grew to love the smells that increasingly permeated the car as we made his rounds. Bendel's iconic black and white striped boxes still elicit warm memories. I especially came to admire Papa Jim's easy manner with the shop proprietors with whom he exchanged multiple "honeys" and "loves." And I enjoyed the flattery that was directed at me by these invariably beautifully made-up middle-aged women.

For thirty years my grandmother had accompanied her husband on his trips – a commitment that seemed beyond the call of duty to some. My grandparents never owned a home and lived in hotels between periodically bunking with my parents. But Grandma was worn down and perhaps in the beginning of her fatal cancer. So that summer I was drafted as her substitute.

Our first calls were in Atlantic City which contained so many customers that we stayed several days. They were the first days (and nights) of my life when I was totally free and unsupervised. I spent hours exploring the Atlantic City Boardwalk. It was there that I discovered the beauty of the nude female form. At age sixteen, long before the advent of PLAYBOY magazine, my first exposure was the 25 cents-in-the-slot that allowed a vision of flipping cards simulating a moving picture. Low tech certainly, but highly exciting to a virginal boy.

One night I watched the diving horse at the end of the Steel Pier. A young woman astride a blindfolded horse would mount a high platform and step off down into what seemed to be a very rough sea with ten foot swells rolling in from the Atlantic Ocean. Amazingly both horse and rider soon bobbed up alive.

Around midnight I was in the Steel Pier ballroom listening to the orchestra of the left-handed violinist Johnny Long. Pop music was a bit more harmonious and sophisticated in those days. While I was standing listening on the sidelines, several girls even asked me to dance. Perhaps I looked older because I was dressed in a tie and sport jacket typical of 1950. In my era, teenage boys wanted to look more mature; in dress today they seem to prolong childhood. Even at age sixteen I loved ballroom dancing and so we swayed to the sounds of Long's theme song, "The White Star of Sigma Nu."

Later, when I returned to my grandfather's hotel room, he was asleep, but the room smelled of some alcoholic drink. It was an odor with which I was to become very familiar. Everything deteriorated as we moved north. Papa Jim's customers came further apart; accommodations sank from $20 hotel rooms, to $10 motels, to $5 cabins where I had to insert a quarter into the TV every thirty minutes in order to watch Eddie Lopat pitch for the Yankees. Cash was running short as more was consumed by Papa Jim's drinking and my quarter deposits.

If Atlantic City was near heaven for me, Salamanca, New York was akin to hell. In 1950 it was a railroad town. The yard tracks seemed to run right down Main Street with bright lights and switching engines present all night. Years later when I read Dante, his INFERNO reminded me of my visit to Salamanca. Alas, I met no pretty girls. Rather I became acquainted with a rich assortment of hard drinking bars. Several times I had to walk into some saloon filled with off duty railroad men downing their boiler-maker hits of whiskey and beer, then lead Papa Jim back to our room to buck him up for the next day's calls.

With his gift of gab, my grandfather was quite popular in the bars – at least up to the point when he would pass out. Patrons would help me get him to the car. In later years I became aware of an anomaly about those bars where Papa Jim would drink with an ethnically diverse crowd. I had recovered him from dark dives in some quite scary neighborhoods. Once I was sent into a City Park tavern to call him home to my parents. He was there swapping baseball stories with his fellow black drinkers. But he was a man who, when sober, possessed a truly astounding prejudice. A transplanted Canadian, he had once lived in Atlanta and affected a pre World War II Southern attitude toward Blacks: he turned against Harry Truman when HST integrated the U.S. and never attended another Yankees game after they signed Elston Howard. When drinking, however, his prejudice evaporated. What did drink do? Make him a better or worse person?

James Arkels

Our trip eventually ended. I drove us home without a speeding ticket or accident. In spite of its horrors I returned quite proud of myself. Papa Jim had entrusted his life to me (albeit perhaps unthinkingly). Still I had been treated as an adult colleague and I had not let him down. Indeed, I had literally picked him up several times. I vowed that no one would ever have to do so for me – a promise that I've kept. And I've striven to treat all people as individuals rather than members of a category. So perhaps Papa Jim's legacy made me a better person. In some ways he had a stronger impact on me than my father. Papa Jim took me to New York Yankee baseball games and on one glorious summer day in 1946 we watched a home run contest between the Yankees and the Red Sox. In spite of big names like Joe DiMaggio and Ted Williams, the winner was Boston's smooth hitting but aging first baseman Rudy York. Today I frequently walk by Henri Bendel's Fifth Avenue flagship store and remember that summer of the perfect job that turned into something else.

EIGHT

A Year of Working Continuously

During my junior and senior years in high school I seemed to be working continuously. I was striving to establish an outstanding academic record that would gain access to a prestigious college (Princeton and Williams were my prime targets). Evenings and weekends I worked at a Howard Johnson's restaurant scooping ice cream and occasionally cooking hamburgers and hotdogs while sometimes busing tables (still the best hot dogs ever - due to the toasted buns). It was located on the Boston Post Road midway between New York City and an amusement park in Rye. On weekends, the ice cream counter was chaos. With no queuing instructions, customers screamed their orders to me and my scoopers while we often slipped on the wet floors running from the chocolate can to the rum raison. Years later when I walked into my son's college fraternity house, I was reminded of those sticky floors when my shoes stuck to the Sigma Chi floor (of course, it was not spilled ice cream).

On slower Ho Jo days, I spent hours defrosting, boiling, peeling and deveining crates of frozen shrimp. Their odor stuck to my fingers for days. A shrimp cocktail today can transport me back to the cold room in New Rochelle 60 years ago. But I still enjoy eating them.

I continued at Howard Johnson's during the summer but added another job as a day camp counselor. My high school baseball coach ran the camp which conveyed kids from a beach club in the morning to the Iona School athletic field in the afternoon. On the way the bus stopped for lunch at my Howard Johnson's. So I was there seven days a week.

To top off my hours, over the Christmas holidays I worked at my girlfriend's uncle's print shop, The Modern Press, collating, binding, gluing and stapling documents, I was so happy when the minimum wage was increased to $.75 per hour. Years later when I had graduated from college and finished my military service, I was still moonlighting at the MP to support my wife and three children while I pursued a graduate degree at Columbia University. The firm's auditing accountant Benjamin Rosenbaum proposed that I take over the firm from my wife's aging Uncle Chris. He was incredulous when I demurred because, as he put it, "there is nothing better than owning a family business." He may have been right at the time, but the computer led revolution soon put an end to the linotype hot lead typesetting that was the Modern Press's forte.

It was a joy to have money in my pocket, to be able to purchase gasoline (even if only a gallon at a time) for my 1936 Chevie coupe bought for $70. Very few lifetime experiences have equaled picking up my girlfriend Mary Lou after we both finished work on a Saturday night, I at Howard Johnson's, she at New Rochelle's finest department store, Arnold Constable. She would bounce out of the store wearing her sophisticated salesperson dress and high heels. I was on top of the world.

The Howard Johnson restaurant time provided experiences that I have drawn on many times in career and life. In late spring the Wykagyl Country Club hosted the PGA Goodall golf tournament. I desperately wanted to see Sam Snead, Byron Nelson, Ben Hogan, Cary Middlecoff and the other golfing greats of the era.

But doing so meant missing work. I called my manager, Mr. Welch, to tell him what I wanted to do. He said he preferred that I come in because he had no one to replace me. But I didn't – and felt so guilty about it that I very rarely missed a day of work in the ensuing years. I retired from the active Navy with 90 days on the books having not taken a single day of leave in three years. Not, of course, the best recipe for a healthy life.

Nonetheless, I fondly remember the excitement of the day's round and seeing Roberto De Vicenzo victorious in a great upset. Late that summer I was sworn into the United States Navy and commissioned as a Midshipman. I went off to college as an engineering student. At least I was used to endless work, which certainly continued at Princeton.

NINE

Joining the Navy

U.S. Navy Midshipman 1952

Ninety Church Street in Manhattan, New York City has been an iconic site where hundreds of thousands of young men and women volunteers and draftees have been inducted into the Armed Services of the United States of America. For me it was on my 18th birthday in 1952 when I was sworn into the United States Navy. It was an exciting experience because I was just old enough to remember sitting in a movie theater in the early 1940's watching a Pathe' News feature of young draftees being sworn in to confront the Nazi and Japanese challenge.

My parents had driven me into the city from our suburban home in New Rochelle. I was a bit in awe (and perhaps envious) of the young men around me who appeared to be handling the big day on their own. I had been awarded a coveted Naval Reserve Officers Training Corps (NROTC) scholarship that would pay my full college tuition in return for a commitment of one day a week during the school year, three eight week summer deployments, active duty for three years, plus seven years in the ready reserve. So I was no longer subject to the draft and not heading to the Korean War. Nonetheless, we were warned that if we didn't maintain our college grades we would be immediately called to active duty as enlisted seamen.

After our swearing in, I received a physical examination and numerous inoculations for unheard of diseases – an experience to be repeated too many times while sailing around the world. Of particular concern that day was my body weight: one hundred twenty four pounds was the minimum allowed for my five foot, eight inch height. Stuffing myself with Milky Ways, I cleared the hurdle by three pounds.

A month later I found myself as a midshipman on an extremely hot Princeton University football field learning how to take orders from a Marine drill instructor who didn't seem to realize that I expected to be trained as a future Admiral Nimitz rather than a Marine grunt. Just before that simmering day, my parents had driven me to New Jersey for my move in. I still regret my behavior that day. So anxious to be on my own, I ignored them all day and even was embarrassed by their presence.

I survived the following nine months without being sent to Korea so in June 1953 I took my first solo long distance train ride from New York's Penn Station to Norfolk, Virginia. Saying goodbye to my parents late in the evening seemed like the end of my childhood. And so it was because except for short visits, I never lived at my parents home again.

Arriving at the U.S. Naval Base and boarding the U.S. Iowa (BB61) at 0500 (5:00 am) was like revisiting Salamanca. It was incredibly hot and noisy. Built long before the introduction of shipboard air cooling, the Iowa was a World War II vessel whose only antidote for the July below decks heat was the incessant sound from the giant blowers bringing

USS Iowa BB61 in 1953

stifling Tidewater humidity into the 45,000 ton ship's bowels.

I was conducted to the small compartment that was to provide my only private space for the next two months. As I had arrived early, I was given a choice of which of the three high bunks I preferred. By blind luck I chose the top rack giving me just eighteen inches below the overhead (ceiling). But no sagging bottom above me would ever be a nuisance. And I came to feel almost comfy in my tiny space. Being on top, however, made it more difficult when we were ordered to "air bedding" by dragging our mattresses topside to lay them on the ship's life lines.

Being early became a critical element in maintaining my sense of control and individuality. I trained myself to wake up thirty minutes before reveille so I could get to the head (bathroom) to wash and shave before the mass of my new shipmates. Especially appreciated was not having to sit cheek to cheek on the public trough that served as the toilet – thus evading the thankfully occasions when some jokester would float a lighted chunk of paper that would pass below the several exposed tender bottoms.

If my own sleeping compartment was hot, my first watch station was even worse. My assignment was to maintain the water level in the number two engine condensate pump. I had to watch the level in a glass tube, opening and closing a water intake valve as needed – a boring job, but one of high importance in a manually operated warship. Letting the water level get too low could disable a main boiler and steam turbine engine, virtually stopping the ship. The heat and noise generated by the boilers and reduction gear was beyond belief. But one learned to acclimate and stay awake.

Years later when I become an officer, I was assigned to serve as a judge for the court-marshal of a nineteen year seaman who had fallen asleep while manning the same valve on another ship. The chief of his watch had tied the sleepy sailor's shoe laces to the deck grating before yelling at him to wake up. The unfortunate young man jumped and fell on his face. Remembering my own experience at the boring job, I felt some sympathy for his plight.

Luckily for me, my second watch station training was in a happier location – on the eleventh level above the main deck way up in the superstructure. I was the forward port lookout. With my (heavy) binoculars I would scan the horizon in ten degree increments earnestly looking for something threatening or at least interesting enough to report to the bridge. Visions of spotting a half hidden rocky shoal or a submarine's periscope wake danced in my head.

My general quarters (battle) station was as far from my lookout post as one could get to into the bowels of the Iowa's hull. I was the lower right powder hoist operator in the second of three sixteen inch gun turrets. I loaded six 60 pound silk encased bags of black powder into the hoist for each firing of the gun which could send a 2000 pound shell up to fifteen miles. I was so far below the ship's waterline that the sound of the guns firing produced only a muffled roar and shuttering of the hull. Many years later, my successors were very unlucky when the same gun exploded killing everyone in the compartment.

TEN

A Finnish Girl in Sweden

Stockholm, Sweden

During the summer between junior and senior college years I was assigned to an Atlantic Fleet destroyer. It was the last sea opportunity to prepare us Midshipman for our soon to come commissioned officer status. In the days of big military and budgets and Cold War flag showing, we cruised to a number of delightful ports including Bergen, Norway and Stockholm, Sweden.

I saw Ritva in the Bergius Gardens Botanical Park in Stockholm and it was a clichéd but real jolt of lightening. Not a classic Swedish blond, she had dark hair with a delightful ski jump nose. She was not Swedish, but a Finn – with just a hint of Laplander. She was wearing a black turtle neck sweater in the cool summer evening while I was in a blue dress uniform. In 1955 an American military uniform was still a draw, but I thought the attraction was mutual. We clearly wanted to spend as much time together as possible in the days that my ship would be in port.

Ritva invited me back to her apartment. In itself this was a novelty for me because at age twenty I didn't even know any American girls who were self supporting with their own apartments. She made coffee by simply boiling the beans and water together in a sauce pan. At the time I was still not a coffee drinker, but to me it tasted like ambrosia. My liberty expired at midnight so I had to return to the ship. When I got back, however, I was able to trade places with another Midshipman whose liberty didn't expire for twenty four hours.

I returned to Ritva's apartment in the middle of the night. We talked, kissed, necked and began what in those days was called petting. I was surely a novice having never even unhooked a girl's bra before. Thankfully (in retrospect although not at the time), we both realized that things were going too fast and we stopped. When I left the next day she said what a good representative of the United States I was. I never did quite understand whether or not this was a complement.

For months thereafter we corresponded as I carried her photograph in my wallet. I had fantasies of flying to

Stockholm over the Christmas holidays. All of this was causing dissonance for me because I was also in love with my long term girlfriend Mary Lou. Although not yet formally engaged, I was planning to give her an engagement ring when I could raise the money. So I remained in the U.S. and we agreed to marry the next winter after graduation. I borrowed money from the Princeton's financial aid office to have my grandfather's diamond reset.

I have never regretted not returning to Sweden, but cutting up Ritva's letters and photographs was certainly bittersweet. Years later I learned that during the winter of my uncertainty my future wife had received a marriage proposal from a young physician that she had been seeing. Thankfully, we both made the best decision. I think that we both were very lucky to have had to face those choices. They strengthened our commitment to the ones we made.

ELEVEN

Don't Get Married!

On Commissioning Day, June 1956

When I reported to the USS Cotton (DD669) a week after graduating from college, the Executive Officer strongly urged me not to get married. Explaining how the ship was to deploy for training in the Caribbean followed by a January departure to foreign waters, he argued that the combined stress of the Navy and a new marriage would be burdensome. I later discovered what a playboy the XO was so perhaps he had really been warning me about how much "fun" he thought I would miss in the various exotic ports we would be visiting (or if I didn't miss the fun, how guilty I would feel).

I nodded my head but thought that there was no way my fiancé and I would change our December wedding plan. However a providential alternative soon presented itself. The ship needed an Anti-submarine Warfare Officer so I was given the tough assignment of attending the eight week ASW course in Key West, Florida. Having a chance to spend the fall in Key West, we moved up our wedding date to September, a week before my school reporting date.

There was a complication however. I and the ship would be training in Guantanamo, Cuba until two days before the rescheduled date. My future wife and her mother would have to make all the plans on their own (something I didn't really miss). But the timing almost torpedoed the wedding. Upon my returning from Cuba, we discovered that there weren't enough days between getting the license and the receiving the required blood

Commanding Officer at Wedding September 29, 1956

test results. In panic, my future mother-in-law called a city judge friend who was able to cut the red tape.

Anti-submarine Warfare School was challenging and enjoyable. And it fit my intellectual skills turning out to be the only school where I graduated first in my class. Returning to the ship, my Commanding Officer expressed his pleasure with my performance, but also observed that I was the first groom that he ever seen who had returned from his honeymoon pregnant. My new wife was such a good cook and I so enjoyed the chocolate hot fudge marshmallow sundaes that she made that I had gained twenty pounds in eight weeks.

Luckily, Navy food while I was at sea for the next five months returned me to normal weight. My new bride, however, put some of my lost inches onto her waist. When I returned, she was five months pregnant.

During my three years of active duty, I was away more than home. Lengthy deployments to Europe and the Middle East created wonderful experiences for me, but were accompanied by a terrible longing to be with Mary Lou. Coming home was always glorious. Looking back all these years later, I believe the separations created a permanent appreciation for the gift of time together. I frequently traveled on business in later years and every short separation rekindled the passion to be home.

TWELVE

Absent from Five Births

Pregnant Mary Lou, Newport, RI 1957

In today's meaning of the word "present," I was not present at the births of our five children. With the first, I was at sea with the US Navy on a blacked-out mission so outgoing communications from the ship were forbidden. Our first born was past due date and I had to leave Mary Lou around midnight to take a train from Stanford to Newport. We set sail at 0700 and later that morning the ship received a message of Sarah's birth in New Rochelle. I couldn't even send a message acknowledging her arrival. Luckily, I had a supply of cigars to distribute. She was three months old when we returned and I saw her for the first time.

With the births of the middle three Judith, Gregory and Jennifer in 1960, 1961 and 1964 respectively, I was in the hospital, but isolated down the hall in the then traditional the father's waiting room. So no delivery room photographs, video tapes or digital recordings are available – and not missed by me. Our last born Stephen was born some years later in 1973 in Philadelphia when I was away teaching a summer course in Hanover, New Hampshire at Dartmouth College. A messenger came into class announcing the happy event. I got a rare ovation from a class. I remember remarking to the students that I was worried that I would be sixty two years old before he would graduate from college. It seemed unimaginably old. But he made it and so did I.

It is easy for me to say, but all these births seemed so "easy." Being absent of course disqualifies me as a commentator on what my wife went through. Nonetheless, given the blessedness of memory loss about pain, even Mary Lou will agree that her births were remarkably quick and easy. When our oldest daughter was having her first child, she was shocked at how many painful hours it took. She good naturedly chided her mother for misleading her to think that childbirth was a lark. In my absence, a sixteen year Sarah had accompanied Mary Lou to the hospital for her younger brother's birth. She had barely dropped her mother off and parked the car when Stephen arrived.

Mary Lou and I did endeavor to convey to our children that life and parenting were "easy" and joyful. We certainly didn't intend to mislead them or be overly protective, but we did enjoy each other. And Mary Lou had this wonderful knack of turning difficulties into games. She could defuse almost all stressful situations.

THIRTEEN:

An Uncertain Faith

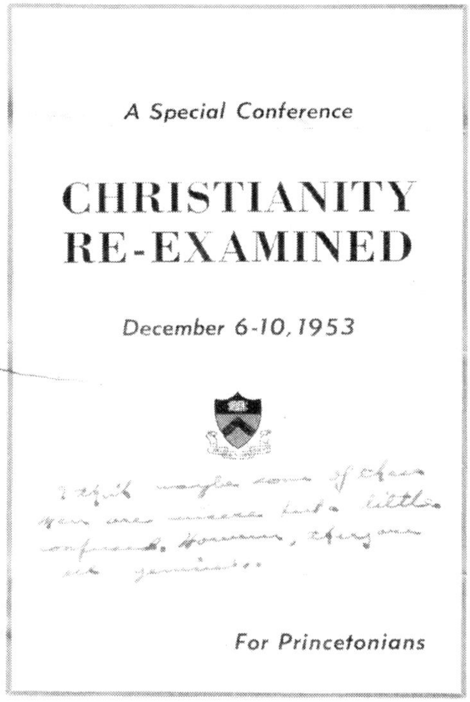
A Special Conference

CHRISTIANITY
RE-EXAMINED

December 6-10, 1953

For Princetonians

I faithfully attend Roman Catholic Mass. I'm not afraid of the eternal consequences if I don't make it, but I feel a bit bereft if missed. This sounds strange even to me because I can't say that I am a Christian believer. Indeed, I am absolutely repelled by Evangelicals who claim Jesus as friend and personal savior. Such claims are so preposterous. My uncertain prayers go out to a more impersonal Spinozan God.

I was baptized and confirmed in the American Episcopal Church. Sunday school was in the fairly high Church, St. John's in Larchmont, New York, where the priests were addressed as "Father." Studying religion always fascinated me. The only academic program other than the US Navy ASW School in which I ranked first was Sunday school (strange bedfellows). I have continued reading about religious history, biblical scholarship, new age concepts and most of the atheistic promoters. Of course religion is absurd and frequently dangerous. Nonetheless, if Man did create God, and not the other way round, it is still one of Mankind's greatest strivings.

I have the highest respect for those who believe and attempt to live their beliefs – except when they try to impose them on others, especially me. During my freshman year in college I attended a campus Protestant revival. Princeton in the 1950's was a place that fostered religious exploration. Its Presbyterian roots still persisted in its compulsory chapel requirement. We were expected to attend weekly, turning in an attendance card found in the University Chapel or, in a liberal gesture, in any town church. A course in humanities with a generally skeptical view of religion was also a requirement. My dorm rooms were filled with religious debate for among my immediate mates were two RC's, one Christian Scientist, one Jew, a Presbyterian, a Lutheran and two non-professing.
While at that revival meeting I told one preacher about my interest in the Catholic Church. My girlfriend was a faithful Catholic whose commitment to her faith was so impressive. Unfortunately, the earnest Protestant cleric responded to my sharing in precisely the wrong

way by claiming that "Catholic girls often make themselves sexually available to Protestant boys to trap them into marriage." Wow! He certainly wasn't familiar with any Catholic girls that I knew. And certainly not with Mary Lou for whom premarital sex was unthinkable.

Unexpectedly, I found studying Roman Catholicism to be so much more intellectual than the Protestant biblical studies in which I had grown up. It was certainly more congenial to me that the emphasis on literal biblical interpretation and blind faith that seemed to characterize the growing fundamentalism. I studied the "Summa Theologica" at the Aquinas Institute in Princeton under a Dominican Father Hugh Halton. I realized of course that St Thomas's attempt to prove God's existence was ultimately inconclusive, but I admired the effort. He appealed to my engineering mind.

In sophomore year I converted to the Roman Church and was confirmed soon after. My confirmation sponsor was one my roommates, Bill Lawlor. Bill was ultimately a *magna cum laude* graduate who went to Harvard Law School. The faith commitment of such an intelligent person was an inspiration to me. I'm sure that I have never approached his depth of belief, but I've sure wished for it.

Three years later I found myself as a Commissioned Officer on the Destroyer Cotten. It was a small combatant and didn't have space for a chaplain. When at sea for an extended period, the Navy encouraged the Captain to arrange services for the various religious groups represented on board. I was the senior Roman Catholic. It fell to me to invite my co-religionists to a prayer service on Sundays. Fortunately, a senior and wise First Class Bosn's Mate of French Canadian extraction was of great help as we arranged services following the Roman Missal's calendar. I have no idea of what proportion of the ship's 250 sailor compliment was R.C., but we usually had a group of twenty or so assembled on the torpedo deck if the weather was good. We would say the Rosary and I especially enjoyed reading from the 46th Psalm:

God is our refuge and strength, a very present help in trouble.
Therefore will not we fear, though the earth be removed, and though the mountains be carried into the midst of the sea;
Though the waters thereof roar and be troubled, though the mountains shake with the swelling thereof.....
He maketh wars to cease unto the end of the earth; he breaketh the bow, and cutteth the spear in sunder; he burneth the chariot in fire.

In a world not supportive of an open display of faith, it took some courage for our young seamen visibly to identify themselves as Catholics by attending. I doubt that even I would have participated if the Captain had not made his expectation so clear.

A psychologist might observe that I resolved my uncertainty about appearing as a Catholic by becoming even more committed and she would be right. Play acting can strengthen the real thing. The teenage sailors in my group at least got to see that a presumably intelligent Princeton graduate privileged officer acted on his faith as many of their parents did.

On April 13, 1957 I wrote to Mary Lou: "I've just come from rosary. We say it most evenings around 1900. Usually, there are about fifteen white hats and myself. It seems a long time since we were together at bed time when you would be kneeling saying your prayers and I would be across the bed touching your hands and saying mine. I may be a poor Catholic, but I am certainly glad that I am one."

In spite of my skepticism, I have experienced moments of transcendence in church that repeatedly offer renewed motivation to continue the commitment and the Sunday walks to Mass with my wife. And I must admit, I really enjoy the complements from fellow parishioners for my singing during the service. We Protestants were taught to really sing the hymns!

FOURTEEN

Finding A Way

Kodak Park, Rochester, NY

The year 1959 was an incredibly fortuitous time to be leaving military service and looking for a job in engineering. I was courted by the elite of American corporations: IBM, GE, Bethlehem Steel, Continental Can and Eastman Kodak. All flew me to various locations trying to sell me on the fit between my future and the firm's. It was a heady experience.

Mary Lou and I would discuss the merits of the different businesses and their `immediate and longer-term locations. Could we live in Endicott, New York with IBM hoping to eventually be promoted to IBM Manhattan headquarters where she had worked after college graduation? Or was Quincy, Massachusetts with Bethlehem Shipbuilding better because of its proximity to Cape Cod? But, would we eventually have to move to Pittsburgh? And so on.

The winner was Eastman Kodak primarily because I loved its image and the product. My father had been a devoted photographer carrying his beloved Leica Camera to work every day. My childhood home was filled with his photos and camera magazines and books. I wanted to learn photography and Kodak offered free courses and dark room facilities to all employees. In addition, we liked Rochester because of its proximity to the Finger Lakes where Mary Lou had attended college. Two weeks after being released from active duty in the Navy, we gave up bunking in my parents' home and U-Hauled to Rochester to a rented garden apartment.

I joined a group of very smart engineers in the Department of Industrial Engineering at Kodak Park. My role had two components: (1) to assist operating managers to run more productive departments by applying industrial engineering methods and measurement techniques; and (2) to design and implement pay for performance incentive systems for individuals, groups and departments. I was not very good at either.

My first mistake was in assuming that operating managers really wanted to change their departments to be more efficient. Many managers were quite happy with how things were going. My suggestions that we might make things better were often seen as an outsider's criticism. But if I sat at my desk waiting for them to call for help, I was often twiddling my thumbs. There were too few calls. Given the times, many managers simply knew they could sell all the film that they made with a markup of some 5-10 times the cost to manufacture. Middle-aged managers felt that this would go on forever – or at least until they retired.

My second error was in underestimating the strength of operating employee's resentment of my setting production standards. Walking around holding my stop watch as a supposed efficiency expert provoked substantially friction. Many of the employees, especially the women who sorted outdated 35mm film roles in order to recover the silver in the emulsions, were very creative with extraneous sorting movements trying to "snow" me into setting an easy quota. They would salt the conversation with observations like:

"Ross, I was in my butcher shop yesterday and peered into the freezer with its ice covered sides of beef. I thought that must be what your heart looks like." They saw me as pushing a speed-up that would reduce the money they had for vacations and gifts for their grandchildren.

The somewhat younger male sorters also were resistant. They wanted to earn money, of course, but just as important was predictability of daily work effort and job security. They sorted large roles of rejected film or returned motion picture reels that varied substantially in ease of sorting. Therefore, they developed methods of "hiding" work on the good days when everything was going well. This hidden surplus was used to augment the count when the incoming product was more difficult. They earned 109% of the expected quota every week and day and even half-day for months at a time. They simply smoothed everything out at a level that would keep management happy, keep me off their backs and provide earning stability. They had no reason to "improve" anything.

All this sorting was done to separate the film from the plastic and metal in which it was packaged so it could be chopped up and deposited in large vats to which were added enzymes that dissolved the gelatin that held the light sensitive silver-halide emulsion. Thus, we freed up the silver for re-smelting and reuse in new film. At $10.00 per ounce it was worth it. This Recovery Room was always hot and humid with a smell not unlike the inside of a human lower intestinal tract. For years I kept a tie that I often wore to work (Kodak still had a white shirt and tie requirement for professional employees!). When things were going badly in subsequent jobs, I would take the preserved tie out of its plastic bag and take a sniff. It would quickly remind me that things could be worse.

My first published journal article after I left Kodak was about this experience and it appeared in a magazine of the American Management Association. I blamed Kodak for its inability to utilize the skills of its young engineers. Unlike the military, I argued, responsibility and recognition for performance came too slowly. I was told that my old department seized all the copies when the publication was delivered. With the passage of time, however, I now realize that it was more me than Kodak. I was too passive. I expected experienced managers to take my advice simply because I was so "smart" and my ideas were so "good". Worse, I was politically naïve, insensitive to the desire of managers and operators alike to put a priority on predictability and stability. I had to learn to sell myself and my ideas.

I began to plan my escape. The first step was to take the GMAT exam and apply to the University of Rochester School of Business masters degree program in Industrial Administration. I started taking two courses a semester along with an incredible cohort of fellow students. Given the population of engineers in Rochester at Kodak, Bausch and Lomb, Haloid Anderson (soon to be Xerox) and Rochester Products, it was not surprising that the GMAT scores were very high – the highest in the nation according to my Finance professor.

I thoroughly enjoyed the academic challenge at a time even while I was becoming more dissatisfied with my Kodak work. This two year period was the most difficult of my adult life. Judy and Greg were born in Rochester in 1960 and 1961 joining Sarah and us in an ever shrinking two bedroom apartment. Judy was born early in the morning in a typical Western New York snow storm after which I went to work. No one took time off in those days; there were no new father's leaves. Greg was born in July when our plans for leaving were being finalized.

I have never believed in praying for God to intervene in human affairs in answer to a personal desire. I have only done so twice in my life and this was the first. For a time I went to daily Mass seeking guidance on what should be my career orientation. No midnight visitation occurred, but I gradually developed the courage to quit my job and apply to various doctoral programs with the aim of pursuing an academic career. I was amazed to discover that one could earn fellowships that would cover the total cost of a PhD program. I applied to Harvard, Carnegie-Mellon and Columbia. Columbia was a clear choice because I was named a Ford Foundation Fellow which included all tuition and a $5000 annual cash stipend. Plus, of course Columbia was in New York City close to New Rochelle. Mary Lou and the three small children flew to LaGuardia on a Mohawk DC3 and I drove a U-Haul loaded with our possessions to start a new phase of our lives. It became a most joyous phase.

It almost ended prematurely however. We rented a flat on the second floor of a very old farm house now in the middle of suburbia. When the days turned colder we noticed ”something” was wrong in our bedroom. Did we smell smoke? Did we feel especially drowsy in the room? Inspection revealed that a chimney ran through our closet and that it was leaking carbon monoxide into the apartment. Fortunately it was detected and fixed. So we bunked our three children on wall to wall beds and cribs in the apartment's “master” bedroom and I set up my work desk in our small bedroom under a tier of book shelves which soon fell on me as the old plaster gave way. Whatever was in those books was certainly pounded onto me, if not into me.

Columbia was a grand success for me. I gained the respect of my fellow students as well my teachers. Very early I was asked to teach a required graduate course called “Conceptual Foundations of Business.”

Columbia Graduation, May 1966

It was a course unique to Columbia at the time and it required a wide range of historical, sociological and business knowledge. I worked like hell, but nobody walked out of the class.

In 1964 I began interviewing for standing faculty positions. I was disappointed that I was not offered a tenure track Assistant Professorship at Columbia, but they only offered one to a graduating Ph.D. student. It went to Boris Yavitz who went on to a distinguished career including Columbia's Deanship. Fortunately, I was recruited by the Wharton School of Finance and Commerce at the University of Pennsylvania in Philadelphia. At the time I visited the campus I had been in Philadelphia only once and never on the Penn campus. I fell in love with all of it. Wharton was the nation's oldest business school, Penn was a Ben Franklin inspired entrepreneurial university in as traditional a colonial city as one could imagine. All seemed to fit me instantly. I joined the faculty at a yearly salary of $9000, the same compensation for which I had started at Kodak five years before.

By the time I formally received my PhD at Columbia's 1966 commencement, our family had grown to four children with Jennifer's birth in New Rochelle in 1964. We all attended the ceremony at which we overheard a graduating college student say to his friend that he was so glad to be leaving so he could now shave off the shaggy hair and scraggly beard which were at that time mandatory for credibility on the Columbia campus. When we returned to our parked car for the trip home, we discovered it had been vandalized with paint splashed over it. We were all happy to be leaving New York City.

That evening I hosted a dinner for parents and relatives at Tarrytown's Tappan Zee Inn on the Hudson River. It was a celebratory affair at which I thanked my parents for their special contributions to my academic success: Mom for her love of books and Dad for his ability to blot out distraction and focus on a task. Unexpectedly, the restaurant refused to accept my brand new American Express Card. I was facing an $900 bill with no cash or blank checks. I thought I would have to wash dishes again, as in my earlier Howard Johnson days. To my amazement, however, Mary Lou's Uncle Frank had sufficient bills and advanced me an instant loan.

Two years later Columbia asked me to return and join the faculty. But, by then I owned a home with a wife and four children so another move was unthinkable.

FIFTEEN

Excess Baggage and a Bad Transmission

Volkswagen Bus 1975

In the spring of 1975 I published a major textbook after receiving a $15,000 advance from a publisher. For the first time in my life, I had some discretionary money in the bank and cash in my wallet. The first thing I did with my new found wealth was to buy my first $100 suit (Hart Shafter and Marx). I felt I had arrived at age 40.

Unhappily, later that spring my nomination for full Professor at the University of Pennsylvania was rejected by the Wharton School Personnel Committee. Unsure of the future, we decided to take a family trip to Europe to celebrate the book and our oldest daughter's high school graduation (and to forget the rejection).

We booked eight economy seats on a flight to London on Lufthansa. What a crew we were when we arrived at the deteriorating shed that was then the Philadelphia International terminal: Ross, Mary Lou, Mother-in-law, and five children aged 17 to 2. Almost immediately after takeoff, I got into a heated argument. Smoking was still allowed in those days, toward the rear of the economy compartment. Our seats, however, were just forward of the invisible boundary. Even then, cigarette smoking was not a problem for us. But the passenger behind me was smoking a very large cigar. And the cabin airflow seemed to move forward. Gently (I thought) I reminded the smoker that cigars were explicitly forbidden. No acknowledgement. He didn't seem to understand me. I suppose he was a German speaker, but I got nowhere. Seeking out the flight attendant, I voiced my complaint politely pointing out that cigar smoking was *verboten.* Apparently the attendant understood neither English nor German because she maintained that smoking was allowed, period. Only thirty minutes out of the United States, I was already seen by most people in the economy cabin as an Ugly American.

Arriving at Heathrow Airport, we piled into our rented twelve-passenger Leland bus for our United Kingdom touring. Luckily the manual transmission shift was in the familiar H configuration so all I had to worry about was sticking to the left side of the roads. Leaving

London, we drove southwest toward Devon from which my great grandfather had emigrated 110 years earlier. Arriving in Chumleigh, we found it a picturesque village where we sipped out first warm British beer. More importantly, we toured the local Anglican Church named St. Mary's. The surrounding cemetery contained many tombstones with my brother's, father's, grandfather's and great grandfather's name: Richard Webber. For this Webber, it was very moving. And I believe meaningful to my children.

The church interior disclosed an even more meaningful ancestor. Back in 1534 in a pique with the Roman Catholic Church over the termination of his unfruitful marriage to Catherine of Aragon, King Henry VIII, the erstwhile Catholic "Defender of the Faith," had seized St. Mary's and expelled the Roman cleric. Searching for a replacement for the new Church of England parish, one George Webber stepped forward to assume the burden. Webber family lure had never passed this tale on to me for whom it had a special meaning. I had been raised in the American Episcopal Church, part of the worldwide Anglican Community where I went to Sunday school and served as an altar boy. Yet, in college I converted to Roman Catholicism. I had felt it as a sort of "return" to the Church so that visit to Chumleigh's Church marked full circle.

After a stay in the gentile poverty of a deteriorating London hotel named the Belgravia, we drove to Dover to take a ferry to the continent. Unfortunately, we couldn't take the Leland to Europe so we had to board as foot passengers - eight people and twenty-four bags. It was a nightmare getting our gang on the ferry. We were reconsidering our whole venture. And it was worse on the other side.

Our ferry docked in Ostend, Belgium where we repeated the chaos of the baggage. And there we sat on a park bench for hours. The Volkswagen bus that I had so carefully pre-ordered was nowhere to be found. It was Sunday and the person answering the telephone spoke Flemish. Fortunately, my wife's college French finally produced the reserved vehicle. Unfortunately, the VW had a faulty automatic transmission, instead of the manual I had requested. The agency had simply assumed that no American would really know how to drive with a manual. The misbehaving transmission cut out the engine whenever we were driving on a downward slope. Later driving in the mountainous Alps became quite hairy and very wearing on the brakes.

While driving southward through France, we stopped one afternoon to have a picnic luncheon in a lovely sunlight dappled grove. After surveying the eight of us around the table, a nearby party of French nuns asked

American Family off to Paris, July 1975

if we were *un familie*? They were simply amazed that we could have so many children. It was quite an irony given the historic stance of the Catholic Church against artificial birth control. And their incredulity certainly presaged the subsequent European population decline.

The French Riviera and Monaco were also on our itinerary. For our teenaged daughters' provincial parents, the pervasive bikinis (and some missing tops) undermined all of our previous exhortations of modesty. My appearance on the beach in a European style man's brief was mortifying to me – and even more so to my children. One evening we had gone to view Monaco's famous casino. My two older daughters were intrigued with the scene of middle-aged, white haired men exiting large limousines accompanied by beautiful young women grasping their arms. My 17 year daughter Sarah then offered her worldly explanation to her younger sister Judy, age 14: "That's what happens when girls learn to put on beautiful makeup!" Appearance is all.

In Geneva, Switzerland we had the luxury of staying in a friend's high rise apartment. It gave us a chance to gaze with wonder at the cleanliness and efficiency of Geneva's stainless steel trash collecting truck. More importantly, we could now wash our soiled clothing in the beautiful basement laundry room. Naively we assumed that the empty machines implied that they were available for use. Wrong. Shortly after completing the wash, the building manager chastised us. A resident had complained that we used the laundry outside of the day and time assigned to our apartment. Thus did we become aware of the fabled Swiss penchant for societal rules.

These rules became even more evident when I inadvertently locked our only set of car keys inside the van. Of course it was raining and the nearest VW agency was a several kilometers away. Several of us made the walk only to discover that I had no documentation entitling me to having the vehicle doors opened. The papers were locked inside. The agency could not help us. After trudging back to our safe and secure auto, I decided to take the law into my own hands. Using my trusty Swiss Army pen knife, I carefully cut the rubber away from the driver side front vent window (they still had these small windows in the

1970's). After retrieving the precious keys, I glued the rubber back in place. For the remainder of the trip I worried that the glass would pop out. No one detected my careful surgery when I returned the vehicle at the Frankfurt Airport.

One of last stops before the airport was at Lake Constance, Germany where we stayed in a lovely historic converted monastery right beside the lake. The Steigenberger Insel Hotel was the most luxurious stop of the trip. After registering and collecting our luggage in the elevator, we started up to our rooms. Suddenly, my two year old partially trained son announced that he had to go "number two." And he did. And somehow it fell out of his underpants with an audible plop on the elevator floor. In what my older children still admit was one of the most graceful and imperturbable moves of my fatherhood, I snatched the warm deposit into a handkerchief before any other guests could board. I was usually better in life's crisis than during normal routine.

By this time we were running low on funds and our oldest daughter was anxious to get home to prepare for her impending departure for college. So we moved up our flight by a day. My daughter's wish was fortuitous because the day before at *Schloss Ludwigsburg* I didn't have enough money for dinner. And my credit card was declined. It was time to go home. Arriving early to return the VW bus, the Hertz attendant remarked how dirty was the vehicle's interior. After two weeks of driving with eight people, I couldn't protest. I was charged an extra ten marks for cleaning.

SIXTEEN

On Role Playing

Dorothy Chandler Pavilion, Los Angeles, CA

When I moved from being a university professor to senior academic administration, I wrote in my journal: "Leadership is composed so much of being calm; not discouraged, of communicating confidence to colleagues." In the midst of a particularly messy university controversy regarding the use of animals in medical research, my university relations office had organized a large alumni reception in Los Angles. In the very venue where the Academy Awards were handed out, over 500 alumni turned out for a gala reception. Outside the Chandler Pavilion, hundreds of animal rights activists were chanting while media people were buttonholing people under the glare of television lights. As I dealt with several small emergencies that arose, an alumna came up to me and said, "You are the most relaxed person I've ever seen." Didn't I wish!

Leadership for most of us involves some dramaturgy in controlling ones emotions and stage managing self-presentation. Some are more comfortable doing this than others. To some idealists, being other than "natural" is anathema. Most young engineers are repulsed by the notion that "playing politics" is helpful for organizational success. Since my graduate business classes included many such people, a common educational technique was to cast them in roles that they might find uncomfortable. In front of a student I would drop a bifold labeled with the name of a character in that day's case. I would instruct them to respond to questions “in role,” not as they personally believed about the situation, but as the named character would most plausibly respond.

Some saw my approach as manipulative and coercive. I plead guilty. When asked why I would put a student under such stress, my reply would be that the most effective learning occurs when one is under stress and one must think and act on one’s feet, so to speak. In some years I was able to cast students in an original play that I had written which we filmed and showed to their classmates. They `then had to defend their in role behavior before the full class. The greatest learning, however, took place before the filming, as I (the playwright/director) and the class actors argued about how to interpret my script. I felt like a Hal Prince.

Alas, the technique was too time consuming and expensive to extend to all students.

I came by this approach from my acting experience in high school. It was all too short because I got caught up in trying to be macho by earning athletic letters. At five foot eight and 127 pounds, this was not the wisest choice. Nonetheless, I did get to play a number of roles, the most valuable for my later life being those of an unsympathetic character usually imprisoned by some self or organizational imposed constraints. George Kittredge in *THE PHILADELPHIA STORY* is one such character. An insufferable workaholic prig, he is incapable of understanding Tracy Lord's vivacity and energy (Katherine Hepburn in the film). At sixteen, I played George with little understanding of his working class animosity toward the rich – an attitude that he was unable to control because he was a moral snob looking down on the upper class. So many echoes of George come to me as I hear the words of the 99 percent "Occupiers". George's gift to me was to warn me about my own moral pretensions when confronting people less open minded or democratic than I liked to consider myself.

An even more straight jacketed role is Robert Cauchon Bishop of Beavais in George Bernard Shaw's *SAINT JOAN.* I played the Bishop at age 14 with as austere a countenance as I could muster. Clothed in a black robe, I condemned Joan to the fiery stake without a shred of understanding for the power of her faith. Yet, the role forewarned me against intemperate judgment when confronted with what I considered transgressions by my children. Most of the time I was able to stifle premature condemnation and leave open the time and space for I and my child to bridge our differences. No Bishop I.

I did play male leads in two productions. In *THE BELLE OF BARCELONA* I was the toreador who sings to the 13 year belle leaning over her balcony balustrade. Our audience consisted mainly of elderly residents in the Osborne Nursing Home. But, I could sing on key and they loved me. No one ever had an easier house. In a then more contemporary comedy, I played the high school heartthrob in *TEEN MAGIC*. I particularly liked this eighth grade role because I got to wear a sports letter jacket and pose as a school jock. It took me three more years to win a real varsity sports letter, and then only as a second stringer.

One of the lifelong benefits of childhood acting is learning to appreciate the dramatist that created the vehicle you were in. The experience can extend to all of their other creations. In our seventh grade *HMS PINAFORE*, I played Raf Rackstraw, the wellborn misplaced infant grown to a lowly seaman who discovers his true identity. The real discovery for me was of Gilbert and Sullivan. Later, seeing Martin

Greene play Sir Joseph Porter in a D'Oyle Carte revival added new richness to my earlier exposure.

In retrospect I wish that I had stayed with the stage rather than investing so much time and effort in interscholastic ice hockey and baseball. I certainly draw on my sports experience as I watch my grandchildren play in today's very serious games. Nonetheless, I found the modest acting skills I picked up to be more useful in my professional life. As a manager/leader one must often conceal one's emotions and a convey a somewhat greater confidence than one feels. Spontaneously communicating one's opinions, judgments, and worries often exacerbates the situation when confronting difficult challenges. Being "authentic" is not always the best policy.

SIXTEEN

Why Was I Usually Second?

New Rochelle High School Sophomore Class Officers:
Zaccagnino, Webber, Foradora

I have spent more time in "Vice" than most police. I have often wondered why I have been elected to Vice President or Vice Chairman of so many entities rather than the rare presidency - usually a bridesmaid, seldom a bride. Surely I can't complain that I have been given many opportunities to serve and lead, but usually in a supporting role.

My first opportunities were in high school where I came in second in four consecutive class elections. Such adolescent elections of course are generally popularity contests so I guess I was pretty popular. High school popularity is tinged with some old fashioned group identifications even if one is not sure of what group voters identify you with. New Rochelle High School in suburban Westchester County, New York was a large exceedingly diverse institution. As E.L. Doctorow's novel RAGTIME so powerfully portrayed it, New Rochelle was dominated by old money WASPS and fast rising Jews. In addition, there was a long time African-American community along with Irish and Italian-American areas. The socio-economic diversity was also wide, from wealthy professionals and entertainment moguls in the north end to the Italian dominated West New Rochelle and the Black areas on Lincoln Avenue and City Park. When we 1950's graduates get together, we often express gratitude for the wonderful opportunity we were given to operate in a multi-cultural world that seemed then to work so well. Of course, there were hidden tensions that overtime became more evident, but we learned to generally respect the viewpoints of others.

I lost the class officer races all four times to Dominic Zaccagnino who was from West New Rochelle. Dom was a handsome young man with a warm personality who excelled in basketball and baseball. Indeed, as a catcher on the baseball team, I caught him in many games. I can still feel the sting of his fastball in my left hand. No exit polls existed in these elections, but I think I had the support of the more affluent WASPS and Jews, but little elsewhere. It didn't help that I was a slow to mature boy who weighed 124 pounds while Dom looked like he could be my father. He certainly had more of what the military called "command presence."

One high school organization in which I clearly was on the Presidential track was Tau Pi, my high school fraternity. As a junior I was the Vice President and the fraternity discriminated against almost all non-WASPs. I am ashamed now to admit that it had a constitutional clause barring Blacks, Jews and Italian-Americans from membership. Remember that this is 1951. I thought that this exclusion was wrong and so in my junior year I began a push to amend the constitution to remove these restrictions. Alas, I misread the willingness of my brothers and adult alumni to support change. My initiative attracted little support and a new coolness was directed my way. I had dramatically overestimated my popularity. Consequently, I received little support for the fraternity presidency my senior year.

To my lifelong regret I did not resign from the group. I must have feared an imagined loss of status and friendships if I withdrew. However, it taught me the danger of a leader getting too far ahead of the causes his followers are willing to support. Such rejection can push a leader toward excessive conservatism in subsequent official roles.

My strongest high school constituency was with the most academically talented, those classmates who shared the most advanced college prep courses. I was elected President of the National Honor Society as a junior and named Chief Justice of the Student Honor Court. Not much leadership was involved as I mainly had to look ceremonial. Nonetheless, I gave inaugural speeches on "Knowledge is Power" and "To Whom Much is Given, Much is Expected." If I had gone into the legal profession as an adult, I surely would have become an "activist" judge.

Years later, an academic search consultant approached me about becoming a candidate for Vice President of Development (fundraising) and University Relations (alumni and public relations) for the University of Pennsylvania. I did so and was offered the position by a then new University President. In spite of some Penn alumni reservations about my being a Princeton graduate, most people thought that I was a grand success in fund raising and university communications. During my tenure, Penn moved from 15th to 7th in funds raised among all US universities and won both the National Council of Support for Higher Education (CASE) award for sustained alumni giving and the US Steel award for best alumni communications.

(215) 898-5169

ROSS ARKELL WEBBER
Vice President for Development and University Relations

Franklin Building I-6
3451 Walnut Street
University of Pennsylvania
Philadelphia, Pennsylvania 19104

Several schools approached me during this time to ask if I would be a candidate for their presidencies. Meeting with school search committees can be a secretive process. Most committees don't want their faculty or administrators to know with whom they are talking. And most candidates prefer privacy so their possible rejections don't become public knowledge. One search consultant called me on the telephone with the greeting, "Scarf, this is Cowboy." These were the radio call signs of my ship and the flagship of my 1950's Newport, Rhode Island based destroyer squadron. Unfortunately, I failed this first test and wasn't invited to the later ones. The school wanted someone from the Liberal Arts, not a former engineer and economist like me. Association with the corporate world was a no-no.

I met with another headhunter in a NYC hotel who couldn't see how I, my wife, five children and mother-in-law could live in the President's West Side

Apartment, even though the organization was willing to pay a $6000 monthly rent. I made it to the finals of a New England college but screwed it up when I argued that its business school should be training its graduates to move easily between private enterprise and the national government. One especially conservative Dartmouth alumnus on the committee (who to that point had seemed to be sleeping) burst forth with a criticism that I seemed to be advocating SOCIALISM! Alas, the invitation went to a Harvard administrator.

I keep as a souvenir a letter from Pennsylvania State University asking if I would agree to be considered for its presidency. Given the recent scandals in State College, perhaps I was lucky to decline the invitation.

THE PENNSYLVANIA STATE UNIVERSITY
203C OLD MAIN
UNIVERSITY PARK, PENNSYLVANIA 16802

University Presidential Search and Screen Committee

March 3, 1982

PERSONAL AND CONFIDENTIAL

Dr. Ross Webber
574 Warwick Road
Haddonfield, NJ 08033

Dear Dr. Webber:

Your name has been suggested as a possible candidate for the presidency of The Pennsylvania State University. The Presidential Search and Screen Committee is in the process of collecting information about individuals who might be considered for the position. We would appreciate having a copy of your vita. At this time you need not make a declaration of interest in the position. All information will be held in strict confidence.

If you have any questions, please do not hesitate to call me at (814) 865-9561. We are looking forward to hearing from you.

Sincerely,

Robert S. Friedman

Robert S. Friedman
Chairperson, Presidential
Search and Screen Committee

My involvement with the business world eventually led to my being elected to the Supervisory Board of Arcadis NV, a Dutch based international engineering firm. After some years I was elected Vice Chairman. Like many vice presidencies, my main duty was to be prepared to replace the Chairman if illness or other emergencies prevented his attendance. Unfortunately, I did have to step in for an extended period and I did a terrible job. Chairing the joint board – employee works council was a particular awkward chore for me. Having sat through numerous such meetings in the past, I just didn't see what they accomplished. It seemed to be empty ritual. The employee participants, however, took it very seriously. So when I commented with ill-chosen words that their desire to have veto power over certain management decisions was illegitimate and not in either the firm's or their long-term interests, I was shocked to hear me criticized for my wanting to "Americanize" the company. *Moi,* who always considered myself to be a participatory leader! As my wife subsequently pointed out, I was really a closet authoritarian. I just wanted a clear chain of command and with sharp decision responsibility. Needless to say, I was never asked to become permanent Board Chairman.

After retiring, I ran for President of my Princeton class of 1956. Alas, I came in second again, but did get to serve a deeply satisfying five years as vice president.

In thinking about all these number two positions, it appears one of my weaknesses was political. I just didn't accurately access the political climate in which I was operating. In general, I was in too much of a hurry to get things done. I was too much the **engineer** trying to move in a straight line from problem to solution, from point A to B. One very successful university president for whom I once worked as an assistant told me that I tried to move in straight lines while senior leadership is more like a helix ever advancing and retreating but continuously moving toward a desired future state.

I think now that my greatest weakness was an excessive inclination to compromise when engaged in negotiations. An experienced executive suggested that

I was too “soft” when confronted with unhappy others. Therefore, people considering me for a top position may have been concerned that I would be “too” compromising when representing their organization. Their concern was legitimate.

Nonetheless, as I write I have just completed three very successful years successively as Program Chair, President-Elect and President of the University of Pennsylvania Association of Senior and Retired Faculty. With no modesty, it appears that I finally got most things right.

EIGHTEEN

Writing is the Only Thing

Management Text Book 1975

Gloria Steinem once said, "Writing is the only thing that I do that when I'm doing it I don't think that I should be doing anything else." I identified with that thought and it once torpedoed an appointment to the Harvard faculty. Five years into my Assistant Professorship at Penn, I was invited to give a lecture at Harvard Business School. I had been sharing my research with a Harvard Organizational Behavior icon, Paul Lawrence. In my naïveté I thought I was just making a scholarly visit. In fact they were considering me for an appointment. After making my presentation to an assembled group faculty, I was interviewed by the Associate Dean for Faculty Roland Christianson, perhaps the leading case method teacher of his time. If I wanted a Harvard position, I then made a mistake.

In response to the Dean's question about what I most enjoyed in academia, I said "writing." Now Harvard like other research universities does value publications, but their emphasis for young faculty is on teaching.

They take longer to make tenure decisions than peer institutions in order to give more time to develop one's teaching skills because their traditional case method is not an easy style to master. My excitement about writing seemed to be at odds with what Harvard Business School wanted of me. I did not receive an offer.

This non-event proved a great boon to me. The Penn culture at the time emphasized personal autonomy and achievement. Unlike Harvard Business School, very little teaching was done in teams. Once I mastered my course syllabus I had substantial time to write. Articles and books flowed – thirteen books in total before I retired.

In the pre-computer era I wrote the first draft in longhand. Striving to decipher my ill formed cursive handwriting, I would then type it. Even with my Remington electric typewriter, it was slow and painful.

The key to writing text books back then was an extensive file of articles and newspaper clippings. Endless hours were spent in the library reading journals and Xeroxing copies of promising articles. My file grew to twelve large file cabinets carefully sorted by research and class topics. They provided the footnotes, footnotes, footnotes - ninety pages of them in my 1975 Management text!

It was a miracle when I acquired my first Apple Macintosh in 1986. For the first time I was able to compose at the keyboard. And editing was so much easier. Revising, deleting and moving sections took much less effort than in the previous scissors and thumbtack era. And then the internet arrived, virtually ending those days cutting newspapers.. Time in the library stacks was sharply reduced.

In the pre-computer years, department secretaries were available to transcribe a professor's handwritten script (and sometimes audio tape) into a typed manuscript. In my first teaching position at Columbia University, a typist was available for every two to three faculty. By the time I retired from Penn, there were no typing staff. All of the manuscript typing was done by faculty themselves, and they preferred it.

The flow of words in the pre-computer era was not easy. Handwriting clarity varied so widely that sectaries tried to avoid certain writers by placing their submissions at the bottom of the in-box. With modern education, younger faculty had pretty much lost the skill of cursive writing. So, both faculty and staff were saved by the computer and associated printers. But the secretaries were "saved" right out of the business. Their jobs disappeared.

The OPEC oil embargoes of the 1970's broke the illusion of American economic invulnerability. The winding down of the Vietnam War, the demise of the military draft, long lines at gasoline pumps and the appearance of Japanese cars on our streets all contributed to the fading of the 1960's anti-business counterculture. Applications to business schools soared and the academic qualifications of students interested in business studies improved dramatically.

A happy result of this development for me and other young scholars was that I was recruited by publishers to develop text book manuscripts. I and my wife were courted at New York dinners by Harper Collins; the President of Richard D. Irwin flew from Illinois to entertain us in Philadelphia; and Scott Foresman flew me out to Chicago. It was all flattering – and eventually financially rewarding.

With visions of Nobel laureate Paul Samuelson's ECONOMICS classic dancing in my head, I signed with Irwin, received a $15,000 advance and retreated to my converted laundry home office to produce a

648 page book that was published in 1975 as MANAGEMENT: BASIC ELEMENTS OF MANAGING ORGANIZATIONS. I was very proud of it and even amazed that I had been able to do it. Some Wharton colleagues, however, warned me that a textbook would not be rewarded with academic promotions. Financial success was seen to compromise scholarly research. One professor predicted that I would never be promoted because "your books are too easy to read." To my surprise, the following April the Internal Revenue Service expected a cut of the advance. I had considered it a loan; the IRS counted it as income.

MANAGEMENT was aggressively promoted by Irwin with color printing, mailings posters and drink coasters (I still have dozens). It sold well with two later editions and was translated into Polish. It funded a family trip to Europe and the down payment on a shore house in Stone Harbor, New Jersey.

How people manage their time has been a focus of much of my writing. I was signed by Simon and Schuster to convert my doctoral thesis into a book about managerial time management. They wanted the research translated into practical management advice. I thought I did a good job, but my editor was "disappointed" for reasons that were never clear. The book was rejected. It was subsequently published in 1972 by Van Nostrand Reinhold as TIME AND MANAGEMENT. It sold OK, but never made any best seller list.

My second trade book, however, did make some best seller lists. I submitted the manuscript to the Free Press under the title "Breaking Your Time Barriers," (note the clever illusion to the sound barrier of supersonic fame). To my surprise I discovered that although I controlled the content, the publisher's marketing department controlled the title and cover design. The title as published in 1980 was TIME IS MONEY: THE KEY TO MANAGERIAL SUCCESS (a pilfering of Ben Franklin's famous axiom). The book did cite Franklin, but it was not about him. It was a survey of strategies for managing time with suggestions for translating them into practical steps. The book sold well and was translated into Japanese, Swedish, Spanish and Portuguese.

To give TIME IS MONEY additional life, in 1984 the Free Press bought it out in soft cover under another title: A GUIDE TO GETTING THINGS DONE. Nowhere did the front or back cover indicate that it had previously been published in hard cover under a different title. I didn't refuse any royalties, but I still think my original title was more original. At least the soft cover was cheaper and we distributed to all participants in my two-day Wharton Executive Program, "Executive Self-Management." Giving that program took me to lovely hotels and resorts all over the United States.

The management book of which I am most proud is BECOMING A COURAGEOUS MANAGER: OVERCOMING CAREER PROBLEMS OF YOUNG MANAGERS. Prentice Hall published it in 1991. I tried to offer wisdom to young professionals on how to maneuver through common challenges like leading when you don't have enough authority. Unfortunately, production resulted in a major printing error. Five pages that were to be at the end of one chapter were bound after the first page of the following chapter. I thought it quite confusing, but my publisher argued that "most readers wouldn't even notice." I'm afraid he was probably correct. So much for my priceless prose.

After I retired from the Penn faculty, in 2008 I wrote my first non-footnoted book: a memoir of my forty years in academia as a professor, consultant and administrator: THE DOG ATE MY BUDGET: TALES ABOUT MANAGING AND TEACHING IN THE IVY TOWER. I wrote about some of the humorous, bizarre and ironic situations I had experienced. The idea came from a fun essay I had written for my 50th college reunion. A classmate's spouse suggested I expand it to a book. The idea struck home and I began writing furiously. The past came back and the words flowed.

From my graduation from Columbia in 1966 until recently, I had not been in the main branch of the New York Public Library. Mary Lou and I recently visited to see the restored Rose Reading Room where I had spent time as a Columbia graduate student. It was even more awe inspiring than I remembered. I checked the on-line catalogue to see if it had any of my books. To my delight, the Library had five of them. Perhaps it was not surprising. Nonetheless, I was profoundly moved to find myself in the august company of the esteemed authors collected in that magnificent building.

Unfortunately, just days before writing these words I was in the Fifth Avenue Barnes and Noble where I checked the availability of my latest book INTO THE

RED SEA: TALES FROM A COLD WAR SAILOR. It was listed on their computer, but with a notation of "not in stock." Unfortunately, its absence was not because they had sold them all.

NINETEEN
A Sporting Life

New Rochelle High School Baseball Team 1952

Sports have played a large role in my life. Most of our close friends today in our seventies grew out of tennis groups and competitions in our thirties. My wife and I played doubles against many of them in club tournaments. Although I had played golf in high school, I very rarely played after I became a father. It was just too expensive and consumed too much time. Weekend time with family was so precious that I considered it inconceivable that one would take a Saturday or Sunday to play golf.

Tennis had the advantage of taking smaller time segments. Plus, one gets to hit the ball 500 times in an outing compared with golf's 100 or so. The social events associated with playing blossomed into lifelong friendships and mutual help societies as we aged. Today much of the conversation at our ROMEO luncheons (retired old men eating out) involves college and professional sports. Our wives are even closer with their monthly "Dial-a-Lunch" outings.

When I was a fund raiser for the University of Pennsylvania, I found that my detailed knowledge of sports was a major asset in making contact with a potential donor. Knowing who was playing well or not on local sports teams was often a conversation asset when visiting in New York, Dallas or Los Angeles. I have never understood the attitude of people who denigrate sports by considering interest in them to be immature or trivial. Sports are life and interest in them (like politics) can be a great builder of relationships. My mother-in-law's passion for the Phillies right into her 90's provided me with a great model.

As a boy, the baseball team for which one rooted helped to define you. Our suburban New York community was generally divided between the New York Yankees and the Brooklyn Dodgers. Few identified with the Giants. Our gang thought the poorer kids and non-baseball knowledgeable rooted for the perennial winners – the Yankees. We more privileged boys rooted for the Dodgers because they were always the underdogs.

Rooting for the Dodgers also gave us a chance to display our "liberalism" because they had signed Jackie Robinson in 1947. It was years before the Yankees signed Elston Howard, their first black player. Much later when I was traveling on business, I saw Jack and his wife Rachel in an airport. Contrary to all other past (and future) behavior around celebrities, I introduced myself. I told Jack how much I admired him and how much he had meant to me as a boy. In his kind of squeaky voice, he was very kind in response. I keep a photo of his 1955 World Series champion team on the kitchen wall. Meeting Jack is still a life highlight.

In High School I played varsity ice hockey and baseball. In those days we learned hockey on frozen lakes and ponds but New Rochelle High School had a strong program. Since most public schools didn't field teams, we played private schools from New York and Connecticut. It was thrilling to play Lake Placid High

School in the 1932 Olympic arena. And equally so, to play the US Military Academy plebes at West Point. I was strictly third line on a very good high school team but I made all the out of town trips. It was enough experience that I understand and thoroughly enjoy going to my grandchildren's hockey games. I recently accompanied a grandson to a tournament in Lake Placid in the same arena in which I had played sixty years before. Thankfully, I could still skate.

I was also a substitute on my high school baseball team. Although I started as a left fielder in my freshman year, most of my recreation league experience was catching. That's what I did on the varsity for three years during which I never started a game. My role was to warm up the pitchers and serve as the bullpen catcher. I just couldn't hit a curve ball – nor, to be honest, a good fastball. In all my times at bat, I hit only one fair ball over a fence. I saw the ball leave the park in left field and started into my (only) home run trot when the coach yelled that it was only a ground rule double. The fence was just too close to count as a homer.

Baseball catchers are generally in short supply. Only a few of us are willing to don “the tools of ignorance” as the equipment is termed. I thought I might have a chance to make Princeton’s freshman team. It was March and the outdoor fields were still too muddy so the tryouts were in the poorly lighted Palmer gym. The coach directed me to work with a tall pitcher who had recently signed a $50,000 contract with the Detroit Tigers. He would not be eligible to play for Princeton in his senior year, but he wanted to keep in shape. His name was Dave Sister, the son of a baseball Hall of Famer. I took my squatting position. I caught his first pitch. But I never even saw the second. It was way too fast. It hit me in the solar plexus and I was down gasping for breath like I had been pole-axed. Thus ended my intercollegiate baseball career.

My main sports love was basketball even though I was cut by my high school coach. I was a star on recreation, extramural and church league teams. I often played two or three games a week, usually leading my team in scoring. I once scored 26 points in a 24 minute rec league game. Alas, my tryout for the Princeton freshman team ended after one scrimmage. Playing guard, I faked to my left, dribbled to the right corner and went up for my favorite jumper. The big defensive forward slapped the ball which bounced right off the tip of my nose. I was destroyed. My tears were so thick I couldn't even see anything but the stars apparently circulating around my head. Thus ended my intercollegiate basketball career. I was just too height challenged. Nonetheless, I did play interclub basketball as shooting guard on a team that won the league championship twice.

I coached a couple of my children's teams. My youngest daughter Jennifer was a natural athlete always willing to listen and learn. I concentrated on teaching her to play baseball in hard and soft versions. Remembering that Mickey Mantle's father would stand him against the barn and throw balls at him as fast as he could, I did pretty much the same. I wanted Jennifer to overcome her fear of being hurt. I well remember the day that my hand would sting because her return throws were harder than mine. She had great successes (patting .750 for one season) and I enjoyed coaching her primary school team the "Johnson School Quarterpounders." She went on to star at Penn in field hockey and lacrosse including first string all-Ivy in the latter.

I also coached my two son's town recreation league basketball teams. Coaching grammar school basketball teams is very difficult because the strength and ability diversity of 10-12 year olds is so broad. Defense dominates. Each team had only one player who could really dribble the ball. Dribbling ability is much more critical than height at this level. Because most young boys have not yet discovered the satisfaction of passing off to a teammate who then scores, this meant that the dribbler was the dominant scorer as well. It becomes almost impossible ever to take him out of the game. Without him, our team was just unable to bring the ball up the court. Fortunately, each of my teams had exceptionally talented guards so we won the championships.

One of my dribbler-scorers became a major college player (all Philadelphia Big Five for Penn) and played eight years in the NBA. Yet, I still regret the evening that I didn't take him out of game in which we had a huge lead and he kept dribbling full court and scoring basket after basket because someone had said he was on his way to a league record. Luckily, he wasn't my son so I couldn't be accused of favoritism. My two sons excelled at soccer and rugby, neither of which I knew anything about. Greg was all-state high school soccer at Cherry Hill East High School and Stephen played football at Haddonfield High and rugby at Hobart College.

Mary Lou and I first took up skiing in our 50's. For years we had ferried our children to New Jersey, Pennsylvania and Vermont ski centers. Since we were both fairly good athletes we decided to learn. We never made it to the black slopes, but skied greens and blues all over the East and eventually Colorado, California and British Columbia. Overcoming the fear felt at the top of the mountain is invigorating indeed. Reaching the bottom unbroken is deeply satisfying – a metaphor for life.

Now in retirement with eighteen grandchildren, there is seldom a day when we don't have a choice of which of their sporting events to attend.

TWENTY

At the Theatre

Oklahoma Program St. James Theatre 1944

My mother was an amateur actress from high school through her young married life when she appeared in local theater productions. Her best friend, my father's sister Midge, was a professional actress including playing Nora Charles on "The Thin Man" radio shows. So I was introduced early to Broadway shows: JUNIOR MISS, OLSEN AND JOHNSON'S HELLZAPOPPIN, LIFE WITH FATHER, THE RED MILL and OKLAHOMA back in the 1940's before I was sixteen years old. Alfred Drake and Celeste Holm as Curly and Ado Annie are still fresh in my mind. In 1949, we saw Ray Bolger in WHERE'S CHARLEY and Nanette Fabray and Phil Silvers in the musical HIGH BUTTON SHOES. Fabray was a particular favorite of Mom's so in 1950 we went to ARMS AND THE GIRL starring Fabray and Pearl Bailey. She paid $8.40 per ticket which she thought was outrageous, but they were last minute in a luxury box right over the stage.

Our next door neighbor was the announcer on the radio show, "Fred Waring and His Pennsylvanians" so we were able to attend live broadcasts of the show as well as the first of the late night talk shows, "The Tonight

Show hosted by Jerry Lester". Together my Mother and I jumped up and yelled at the designated times, delighting in making fools of ourselves.

When my girlfriend and future wife Mary Lou came into my life in high school, she fell in love with the theater as much as I. Indeed, she was also an actress in our high school Tower Players who stayed with it and had the ingénue lead Miss Tripp in the 1952 senior year production of THE SILVER WHISTLE. In our teenaged taping of THE PHILADELPHIA STORY she played the wisecracking SPY Magazine photographer Liz Embry (played by Ruth Hussey in the 1941 film). I played Tracy Lord's stuffy fiancé George Kittredge – as unsympathetic a role as ever written.

In high school and college we went to many plays together: Cole Porter's KISS ME KATE, Jose Ferrer in CYRANO de BERGERAC, Arthur Miller's VIEW

FROM THE BRIDGE and DEATH OF A SALESMAN, Jean Giraudoux's TIGER AT THE GATES with Michael Redgrave, and, especially, the adaptation of Alexander Borodin’s music in KISMET.

Encouraged by a high school English teacher, we went to our first opera at the old Metropolitan Opera house on 39th Street . The mezzo-soprano Blanche Thebom starred as Delila in Saint Saens' SAMSON AND DELILA. We had student tickets very high on extreme stage left where I could look right down the front of Thebom’s gown with a full view of her amble breasts. Nonetheless, I did listen to the music and singing. Since then, we have been to many Met Operas at Lincoln Center as well as performances in Philadelphia, Vienna, Venice, Verona, Prague and Santa Fe.

I had neighbor who actually was a Met opera singer – the tenor Jan Peerce. He didn’t know me, but his daughter often drove us to high school in her gorgeous blue DeSoto convertible There was no school busing and it was either taking an indirect public bus with a connection or hitch-hiking the two miles (yes, sometimes we ended up walking, but never barefoot in the snow).

Many years later when I was contemplating retiring from the University of Pennsylvania, some contemporaries were buying places in the sunny south. We decided we wanted no part of Florida. What we really desired was an apartment in Manhattan, preferably on the Upper East Side, a place from which we could expand our exploration of New York's theaters and museums. So we did. And do.

I have experienced so many magical moments in theaters. Here is my top ten list:

10: During his term as Music Director of the Philadelphia Orchestra in the 1980's, Ricardo Muti conducted a concert version of Giuseppe Verdi's NABUCCO. We have seen the staged opera, but it was marvelous to be so close to the stage and to see all the musicians in the concert format. Most of all, there was Muti's magic. No one understood Verdi more than he. And my wife loved the sheen of his black hair bouncing before us as he conducted. We had many wonderful evenings during Muti's tenure at The Academy of Music.

9. Sitting in the audience at the open air Santa Fe Opera one looks westward. One evening, framed against a golden sunset we watched the final scene of Puccini's TURENDOT as Calef sang *Nessun Dorma* followed by his correct answers to the icy Princess's deadly riddles. As the glorious sounds of the final chorus burst forth before the Emperor's throne, the sky's glow deepened from yellow to orange to red and

disappeared. The juxtaposition of artificial and natural lights and colors was astounding – an expression of schmaltz than transcended kitsch.

8. Richard Kiley was a longtime favorite of ours across several shows. As the young prince in the THE KING AND I and as Calif in KISMET, his youthful ardor mirrored my feelings for my future wife. I arrived late from Princeton for a Broadway performance where I was to meet Mary Lou and her mother. They were already seated and I had to remain in the lobby until the end of the first scene, She then came to give me my ticket walking down a flight of stairs dressed in a purple sweater that looked better on her than it would have on Marilyn Munroe. The image is burned on my mind. When I was a few years older, Kiley played Don Quixote in MAN OF LA MANCHA and touched my by then fading idealism to have an important impact on the world. His 1980's portrayal of the father Joe Gardner in the television series "A Year in the

Life" represented the ideal of fatherhood which by then I was trying to manifest in my own life.

7. In the city where it was created by Mozart, we attended a performance of THE MAGIC FLUTE in the Vienna State Opera House. After dinner in the Franz Lehar room of the Grand Hotel, we walked throw the snow to the opera where we were transfixed by the Queen of the Night aria. It was electric - and fearsome. Beyond any other depiction that I've seen since. It seemed to come straight from Mozart's deepest fear.

6. No New Yorker could leave Bobby Short off a list of favorites. We came to him and the Café Carlyle late in his legendary career there. His evocation of Gershwin's New York themed songs captured the glamour, romance and love of the city that Mary Lou and I have shared for sixty years.

5. Although I had seen the original cast of KISS ME KATE with Alfred Drake and Patricia Morrison (and it was wonderful), one performer in the 1999 revival was even more memorial. Marin Mazzey possessed a larger than life boisterous personality perfectly suited to Shakespeare's and Porter's Kate/Lili. Even the great Brian Stokes Mitchell was a bit overshadowed. Some years later, I attended Mazzey's café performance at the Carlyle where I was able to tell her that I had seldom seen a better fit of role and personality than her Kate. Standing next to her, I was surprised by how small she was. She seemed so much bigger on stage as Kate – a mark of a great performer.

4. The two greatest individual performances that I've ever seen were Alice Ripley (2008) in NEXT TO NORMAL and Angela Gheorghiu (2010) singing Violetta in Verdi's LA TRAVIATA. Both left me trembling. Ripley played a disturbed homemaker burdened with bi-polar disorder. Alice's tears for a lost

child and her yearning for a "normal" family were heartbreaking, perhaps especially for those of us who seen the impact of the disease on family life. Violetta also yearns for a traditional family life, but Gheorghiu's performance lifted the hackneyed story into the universal story of "might have been." As the audience left the Met that evening, strangers spontaneously exchanged exclamations of how limp we were from the emotional experience. We knew we had been privileged to be present at a unique event, never to be repeated - even if additional performances remained in the season's calendar.

3. Mary Zimmerman's production of THE NOTEBOOKS OF LEONARDO DA VINCI ends with the aging genius sitting on stage when he hears the beating of a bird's wings. It is death approaching. When pondering his life's successes and failures, lessons learned and unlearned, he suddenly realizes that all the time that he thought he was learning how to

live he was actually learning how to die. It was so touching to me by then in later middle age. I hope I am learning how to also (but not too fast).

2. The Franco Zeffirelli designed interior of the Church of Sant' Andea Della Vaile on the Met Stage surrounded a scene in Puccini's TOSCA in which architecture, religion and music met overpoweringly. The "Te Deum" singing, the priests' incantations, the pealing of the bells, the baritone's lust for Tosca presented a juxtaposition beyond compare. Yes, it was on the edge of excess, but to me it was grand opera at its grandest.

1. My top experience is the first act finale of Stephen Sondheim's SUNDAY IN THE PARK WITH GEORGE where Seurat's mistress is singing about design and the actors are positioning themselves in a tableau of his great painting: "La Grande Jette." As a painter myself, the words about harmony and balance

combined with the music and visual imagery to lift me beyond myself. As a bonus, unlike George in the second act, I was energized to get back to my paints to start another project.

I certainly hope even better theatrical experiences await me.

TWENTY ONE

The Joy of Art

Drawing and painting have been lifelong pursuits. In grammar school I liked it that classmates and teachers thought I had talent. I wasn't in the same league as

Leslie or Sandra, but it was fun. When I was selecting courses for high school freshman year, I first thought I would pursue a commercial art program. Luckily (I guess) I was persuaded to drop art and take Latin and follow the college preparatory sequence. As soon as I had any discretionary money, however, I began buying arts books, especially Abrams Publishing portfolios. By my college years I already had reproductions of many of the popular major artists.

University engineering studies and NROTC left no time for painting, but I did work in a couple of art history courses which I thoroughly enjoyed and for which I earned high grades. So the interest in art was always there. Nonetheless, not until I was in my mid-forties was I able to take time to resume drawing and painting. Like many beginners, I started with a set of pastels and then took a high school evening course in oil painting. My first paintings were of water fowl, often on driftwood collected at the New Jersey shore.

When I began contemplating the reality that I would eventually have to retire, I knew that I was fortunate to already have a passion that I could pursue more seriously. It is much harder to develop a new interest after work stops than to have one already. I wanted to be more knowledgeable and competent about creating art, however, so I began taking continuing education courses at the Pennsylvania Academy of Fine Arts in Philadelphia. Starting with basic drawing, I took numerous evening and eventually day classes in all aspects of figure drawing, still life, and landscape painting. I sat under the elevated I-95 highway in south Philadelphia and painted a neighborhood indoor gun range; I stood in the rain under the Pennsylvania Convention Center overhang to paint a Chinatown corner; I baked in a summer sun on the banks of the Schuylkill capturing the light on the Roosevelt Expressway as it crossed the river. And more time was spent at the Academy drawing nudes in charcoal alternating left and right hands, lines and shadows.

I loved PAFA's traditional curriculum with its emphasis on drawing as the basis of painting. Knowledge of media and craftsmanship were important. In most classes, I was the oldest person in the room. In many, I was blown away by the creativity of a purple haired twenty-something who could visualize the human form so much more imaginatively than I could. We referred to one young woman simply as Michelangelo.

At the end of most glasses, all the students would tack up their work on the wall. Each of us would then have to describe what we had tried to do; what we liked and in what we were disappointed. Our fellow students would then comment. Thankfully, their remarks were generally thoughtful and kindly. My work was never the best, but I generally felt I was above the class average (like Garrison Keillor's fictional Lake Woebegone where every student is "above average").

I incorporated some of this technique into my Wharton MBA classes when I would ask the class to comment on a student's interpretation of the case character whom I had asked him or her to play. Competitive graduate students seemed to accept criticism of their role playing better than direct comment on their personal analysis. In management education, we can only simulate real behavior through cases that describe what some practicing managers did. But in art, the student can actually perform the real action and receive immediate feedback.

Happy Hands: Portrait of Mary Lou 2001

For a long time I couldn't see any unique style to my work until a figure drawing instructor described my drawings of faces and hands as expressing good humored joy. I am now aware that my central ambition is to create beauty on paper or canvas. I am not interested in shock or social criticism. I still am eclectic in media and subject working in acrylics, oil and watercolor. My particular love is urban landscapes where I can combine the geometrical building forms with the exuberant curvilinear nature of trees, plants and flowers. I enjoy juxtaposing a human creation with nature's creations.

When they were painting together, Gauguin once asked Van Gogh why he copied nature and never painted from his imagination. Vincent replied that he could only paint what he saw. But what sight he had! And how imaginative his interpretation of what he saw (indeed, much more so than Gauguin's purely "imaginative" works). I can only paint from I have seen. Luckily, I have been able to travel a good bit collecting sketches and photographs from which I paint when back home. I will not paint a scene from a photograph that I didn't take myself. I generally don't enjoy doing a finished painting while sitting outside in the hot sun or rain.

I often mix media. With urban landscapes on canvas, I paint the buildings in multiple layers of acrylic paint. I love the synthetic medium because of its fast drying and adaptability to multiple glazes. I complete all the building details. I then add the trees and foliage in oil paint because of its ability to cover the acrylic and its blending capability. I feel more spontaneous with oil paint which contrasts with the almost architectural drawing aspect of the buildings (much of which can disappear in the final painting).

Another example of mixed media is combining figure photographs in a water-color landscape on paper. I immerse a photograph of a family member in a landscape where I have photographed them. The idea actually came from a famous J.M.W. Turner painting of a river walk onto which he pasted a little black dog. The finished work creates a dream-like quality that is enjoyable.

I have entered paintings into many juried and no-juried shows at the Markeim Art Center in Haddonield, New Jersey, the Burrison Gallery at the University Club in Philadelphia, and student shows at the Pennsylvania Academy of Fine Arts. I have had two one man shows in which I displayed up to 25 paintings. It is an over whelming experience to be surrounded by one's paintings and to be aware that people are actually enjoying them.

Selling paintings is another matter of course. One watercolor scene of Central Park sold at my last show. And I recently completed and sold a commission of a large waterfront urban landscape. I was thrilled when upon opening the wrapping the client spontaneously exclaimed how she loved it. And then four hours later, she called to say she was sitting in from of her fireplace admiring the new painting hanging over it.

I hope that I may have many more such happy experiences.

TWENTY TWO:

Having Most of It All

Sarah, Stephen, Ross, Mary Lou, Jennifer, Judith Webber 1994

The debate about whether or not a career woman can have it all: job success, marriage, children has been, is, and will be endlessly debated. Undoubtedly, working how some balance is a more difficult for a woman, but men confront similar dilemmas. I certainly did. And any solutions are always temporary, changing with career and parenting stages.

In the early years in the Navy, graduate school and assistant professor, my priority went to job and earning money. In the Navy, one has few choices; you go where you are told according to authority's timing. Graduate school offered greater freedom, but by that time I had three children and getting time alone was precious and critical. Mary Lou and I made a decision to rent an apartment in our home town near her mother hoping she would be able to help out in my absence. Because fellowship money was short, I worked as many odd hours as possible as an all-round sorter, collator, binder and stapler in a family printing business. I was certainly not as involved in infant childcare than most of today's young fathers, especially my sons.

I was thirty years old when I started at the University of Pennsylvania as a Lecturer hoping to finish my doctoral thesis and be appointed as an Assistant Professor. By that time we had four children and the $9000 per year salary that Penn was paying was clearly not going to be enough. Most of my contemporary academic colleagues had none or a single child with a wife who worked outside the home. Because of family demands, as well as my strong motivation to make enough money to avoid the embarrassing credit situations that I remembered my parents confronting, I devoted more time to outside teaching and consulting than was advisable. Or so I was warned. I taught extra courses in the evening school for ten years. I traveled frequently to teach classes for the Philadelphia Police, New Jersey prison wardens, the U.S. State Department, the Army, and the CIA, not to mention assorted corporations like Liberty Mutual Insurance, IBM, RCA and NBC. Even non-for-profits like the Educational

Testing Service, the American Cancer Association, and the American Heart Association paid me for training. As much as possible, my wife and I tried to combine family outings with these engagements. We would pack four children into our Pontiac station wagon and bunk together in a hotel room the night before I would conduct an all-day session in Washington, DC. At $100 for my day's work, we barely broke even. In Palo Alto, California, we all slept together in two king-sized beds for two weeks while I taught for the National Association of Credit Management. These work and family sessions were very tiring, but did provide incredible family memories.

I also wrote text books intended to earn royalties, which thankfully in time they did. All of this writing and outside teaching produced the means to provide by family with the opportunities that I wanted them to have. The effort, however, came with costs. Research oriented universities frown on the path I followed.

Text and popular trade books are simply not valued compared with rigorous; data based research articles in juried journals. And I simply didn't invest enough time in this area to be as productive as my competitive colleagues. I was warned about his and, indeed, I was twice rejected for promotion because of a thin research portfolio. Years later, an older senior colleague told me that I was eventually promoted because I had "administrative potential" – a kind of curse in academe.

Two general categories describe professors: cosmopolitans and locals. Cosmos focus on research and developing an international reputation. They attend numerous professional meetings presenting papers on their research. As a result, the best are offered numerous positions at other schools and often move from campus to campus. In contrast, locals are usually more committed to one institution (perhaps they because they have less outside visibility and receive fewer job inquiries). Locals generally are more active in provided student guidance, serving on faculty governance committees including service as department heads and assistant deans. I played so many of these roles that one fast rising junior colleague resigned because he didn't want to have to do what "Ross does as a full professor."

With four and then five children, my wife did not have an opportunity to work outside the home for pay. Nor did she want to. Because her mother had been widowed at a young age, Mary Lou grew up as "latchkey" child. She didn't want her children to come home to an empty house. Unfortunately, there were times when I was not there and not available to participate in community affairs and sporting events. After playing golf in high school, I didn't play again for twenty years (thus saving a lot of lost golf balls). And I didn't find the time to coach my son's baseball team. He was a good player, but wasn't selected for all

Cherry Hill Township traveling team because (as I later found out) I had not contributed time to the league. And like many young professionals, my friendship group shrunk dramatically. It was ten years after graduation before I attended a Princeton football game or alumni event.

As I came to acquire seniority and security at Penn along with a stable set of income sources, I was able to expand attention to family and social matters, I coached my younger children's softball and basketball teams and attended most of their high school and college games often driving half the night to watch away games. And in time my commitment and loyalty to Penn was rewarded with higher income and promotions to senior positions.

I am embarrassed to recognize that in spite of all the awards and honors that Penn gave me for my institutional commitments, I still resent that I was

Ross and Mary Lou after 50 years of marriage

never awarded a named chaired professorship. The highest scholarly achievement at many schools is recognized with an appointment to a professorship that has been endowed by a donor with a fund used to support the occupant's research. When I walk into the Wharton School and see the chaired professors' portraits on the hall wall, I still experience a feeling of anger. How childish we remain as we age.

TWENTY THREE:

Going My Way

Teaching at Penn 1980

I was playing golf with my son-in-law Ron DePietro. It was not going well for either of us. In frustration, he complained, "Ross, I wasted my boyhood playing cards." I responded, "And I wasted my boyhood in the library." Well, our "wasted" years paid off: he was a vice president of an Atlantic City Casino and I was a professor and vice president at an Ivy League university. Nonetheless, after retiring from teaching I decided to take lessons to improve my anemic golf.

My Korean instructor watched and filmed my swing with exasperation. He then gave me a philosophy of life lecture. With great insight he said, "You appear to be a person who believes that hard work is the key to success. If you try harder, you expect to get better." "Yes, of course," I replied. "Forget it. That's not golf" explained my swing seer. He told me to visualize some despicable character who doesn't give a damn how he does or what others think of him - some guy who looks for the easiest way to do things. "Tom Buchanan" came to my mind. He was Daisy's husband in F. Scott Fitzgerald's novel THE GREAT GATSBY. I've always detested the character for his elite sense of entitlement and for his ill treatment of

Daisy who was an early literary infatuation for me. You can see I took my youthful reading seriously.

I told my instructor that I had a contemptible guy in mind. He instructed me to imagine him addressing and striking the ball as if he absolutely didn't care where it went. In other words, be totally disinterested and relaxed. I tried it and it worked. My golfing sage's point was that the key in golf is to lose one's sense of self; to forget that others are watching; to not care what others say or think about you.

In reviewing my life I realize I too often sought the approval (perhaps admiration) of others. I remember a young Stephen Daedalus in James Joyce's A PORTRAIT OF THE ARTIST AS A YOUNG MAN trying to carry the sacred host safely through Dublin's crowded city streets while being jostled by an uncaring crowd. He was afraid that he would drop it. I fear that I sometimes backed off when jostled. I might have achieved higher positions if I had been more willing to create conflict. Too often I was overly solicitous of others when, perhaps, I was driven more to avoid unpleasantness for myself. Nonetheless, my seeking popularity was generally successful. I collected numerous friends. My wife loves me. My children even like me. All in all, a pretty good deal.

Do you remember ever playing a game of asking what plant or animal you would like to be? I usually saw myself as a cheetah, or my plant as a cattail. What a strange personification. I think I wanted to be ultra flexible, bending with buffeting winds while keeping my roots fixed. No storm could harm me. Lying in bed late at night as a child, I could sometimes hear my parents arguing (or maybe just talking). My room was only a half flight up from the kitchen so I could hear. Or at least I could hear my Mother's sometimes alcohol slurred words. My father spoke so softly that I seldom could make out what he was saying. My Mom fought with words; my Dad with silence. Sometimes I was terrified feeling that hurricane winds were blowing me to and fro. Perhaps my attraction to the Cheetah was the hope that I could outrun my home environment. And in effect, I did.

By the apparent contemporary measures of adolescent development, I was a failure. I never puffed on a marijuana cigarette to get mellow, never snorted cocaine to achieve a high, and never took an amphetamine to improve my SAT score. And I certainly failed at a young boy's paramount high school objective – to lose his virginity. In didn't have sex until I was twenty-two and on my wedding night. I did get drunk once at nineteen at a college party (I will never forget the nausea).

Was I a goody-two-shoes? I suppose so, but in those long ago times, it was so easy to resist temptations that seem so overwhelming to many young people today. It didn't require an especially heroic morality. Nonetheless, the avoidance of youthful mistakes has been so helpful to developing an enduring family relationship. We know each other's history, because it is **OUR** history.

When I went to college I essentially never went home again. As a Navy Midshipman, all of my summers were devoted to training in Virginia, Texas and at sea. Between my Navy scholarship and holiday earnings I never had to ask my parents for spending money. Since the Navy paid for all my tuition and books, I was only dependent on Mom and Dad for room and board while I was at college. And this was a problem because they were often tardy with the payments. Finally, in senior year I went to the Financial Aid Office and borrowed $800 to cover the deficit. It is not a large sum in today's world, but it seemed enormous to me.

In John Le Carre's novel TINKER, TAILOR, SOLDER, SPY, the main protagonist George Smiley thinks: "There is nothing dishonorable in not being blown around by every modern wind. Better to have worth, to entrench, to be an oak of one's own generation. At a certain moment, after all, every man chooses: will he go forward, will he go back?" This collection of tales has looked backward and I have learned much about myself in doing so. Perhaps these lessons will assist me in defining where I want to go now.

I have been much luckier than I thought. On my way, I exaggerated the extent to which my accomplishments were my personal achievement. Being in control (or at least feeling in control) has been a driving motivation. I started out feeling that I did more because of my parents lesser contributions to my effort. I have grown to see what an immature and silly conclusion this was. No, they didn't send me to sports camps, or intellectual development programs, or provide tutors, etc. But they kept a house full of books, repeatedly conveyed me to the library, and shared a love of reading with me. My mother once observed that her favorite activity in the whole world was curling up with a good book and a piece of chocolate cake. I still don't quite believe her, but I certainly share those two loves.

I now realize that my childhood family was not "poor." Actually, we were an upper middle class family whose life style was subsidized by inherited money. It was destabilized, however, by alcoholism, psychological problems, procrastination and poor money management.

I don't know much about my father's relationships with my five siblings. As I've indicated, I didn't have much of a relationship with him. My older brother reports a much closer experience, perhaps because of their shared interest in fishing, photography (and yo-

yoing - my brother was a national champion). I shouldn't blame myself for this, but I could have been responsive to my father’s interests.

In contrast, my mother appears to have forged very strong and unique relationships with each of us. Sitting with me helping me practice the piano while I was in tears, taking me to a movie or a New York show built strong positive memories. Yet, the family links were much less developed. The connections between and among my brothers and sisters seem much weaker – at least in comparison to what others say. The age range among my parents’ children probably contributed to this. My older brother Dick is five years older than I; my younger brother Jim is six years younger; Alan another ten years younger. My two sisters are closer than the rest of us, but twelve and eighteen years younger than me. We generally didn’t celebrate family communications and togetherness.

I was serious and conscientious too early. I wanted to exceed in school so much. I loved being the "smartest guy in the room" (or least among the smartest). It has certainly paid off in career success, But, I was often afraid to be adventurous in fear that I might fail and suffer a setback. Perhaps worse, I was excessively afraid of losing the respect and admiration of peers and authority figures. I wanted to be popular with everyone – a snare and a delusion. I didn't rebel, never "acted -out," and never, ever "f…ed up." I have never regretted this and don't feel I have missed anything. Nonetheless, when I finally began meeting and working with people who were smarter, I did feel a bit lacking in the confidence to handle this situation.

My wife kept all of the letters I sent her while in college and the Navy. This was in the 1950's before e-mail, cell phones and free long-distance calls. Telephoning was expensive so we wrote over 900 letters. Rereading those letters is sobering. I was so active in high school extracurricular leadership positions. At Princeton, I avoided such involvement. I think I was a little shy and lacking in social self-confidence. So many classmates seemed so much more polished (and wealthy – I had to measure everything against what it would cost financially). I did go out for freshman basketball, hockey and baseball, but was cut from all. I auditioned for the premier singing group and was rejected All of this is not surprising for a competitive university. I didn't go out for anything that didn't have cuts. I was just so very busy as an engineering student and a Naval ROTC regular. Both made high time demands on me, especially including morning and Saturday classes and afternoon labs. Intramural sports were the only extra activity that I could justify.

What dominates those college letters is a longing to be with Mary Lou. Rereading them recently, I exclaimed to her, "This guy is nuts, or clinically depressed." My expressions of longing are so frequent and poignant. Was young love really like that? I'm confident now that I was not "depressed," but I am struck by the fact I never complained about the homesickness so common to college freshmen. Leaving home was easy; being away from my beloved very difficult. It appears that I had shifted away from maintaining past family ties to establishing new ones with her. The joy she promised overwhelmed the more uncertain home ties. My college focus became to graduate with an engineering degree with the highest grades possible, to earn my Navy commission, to marry Mary Lou and obtain a professional position with an esteemed big corporation. And it all worked out as planned until I disliked the work at the big corporation.

I sometimes think that I unconsciously tried to recreate my grandfather Richard Jr.'s affluent situation, albeit on a more modest scale. At age 46 I bought a large

Home 1980-1996

white house uncannily like the mansion he had built in 1908. Like his, mine was a large three story, center entrance colonial situated on a corner lot on a small hill that overlooked two streets. A lovely porch was located on the left side. It didn't have the apartment over the garage or a chauffeur or cook, but it had a huge kitchen with three ovens and two ranges. The dining room could seat a large contingent of guests. We often had over twenty at dinner parties. Like him, my mother-in-law lived happily with us for many years. And I enjoyed entertaining at multiple professional, personal and family events. We had three daughters married with tents, receptions, musicians and all. I realize now how much I truly enjoyed being a *Pater Familias*.

My mother thought I took after my quiet father with his shyness. Many years later, she was amazed when I became chief fundraiser and alumni relations officer for the University of Pennsylvania. My job was essentially to be Penn's chief salesman. This amazed her (and, I must admit, even me). My wife and I were recently out to dinner when she observed me opening conversations with the hostess, our waitress, the busboy and the strangers sitting at the next table. She said my mother would have been so proud. Perhaps, I have finally become my mother.

About the Author

Ross Webber was born in New Rochelle, New York. He holds a BSE from Princeton, a PhD from Columbia, and an honorary MS from Penn. He served as an Ensign, Lieutenant (JG), and Lieutenant in the United States Navy. He worked as an industrial engineer at the Eastman Kodak Company before joining the faculty of the Wharton School at the University of Pennsylvania. At Penn he served as a Professor of Management, Chairperson of the Management Department, and Vice President for Development and University Relations. He is now Professor Emeritus and Past President of the Penn Association of Senior and Emeritus Faculty.

Webber was very active in business and management consulting including serving as a Director and Executive Committee member of The American Water Works Company as well as a Director and Vice Chairman of the Supervisory Board of Arcadis NV, an international engineering firm. He is the author of eleven other text and trade books including: BECOMING A COURAGEOUS MANAGER (1991); THE DOG ATE MY BUDGET: TALES ABOUT TEACHING AND MANAGING IN THE IVY TOWER (2008); INTO THE RED SEA: TALES FROM A COLD WAR SAILOR (2011); and TIME FIGHTERS/TIME LOVERS: WISDOM FOR MANAGING CAREERS AND LIFE (2012). He lives in Haddonfield, New Jersey with his wife Mary Louise. They have five children and eighteen grandchildren.

24739378R00127

Made in the USA
Charleston, SC
04 December 2013